THE MISSING LINK

THE MISSING LINK

An Inquiry Approach for Teaching
All Students About Evolution

Lee Meadows

HEINEMANN
PORTSMOUTH, NH

Heinemann

361 Hanover Street

Portsmouth, NH 03801–3912

www.heinemann.com

Offices and agents throughout the world

Library of Congress Cataloging-in-Publication Data

Meadows, Lee.
  The missing link : an inquiry approach for teaching all students about evolution / Lee Meadows.
      p. cm.
  Includes bibliographical references.
  ISBN-13: 978-0-325-01749-5
  ISBN-10: 0-325-01749-2
  1. Evolution (Biology)—Study and teaching (Secondary). 2. Human evolution—Study and teaching (Secondary). 3. Creationism—Study and teaching (Secondary). 4. Intelligent design (Teleology)—Study and teaching (Secondary). 5. Teacher-student relationships. I. Title.
  QH362.M36 2009
  576.8071'2—dc22   2009018397

Editor: Emily Michie Birch and Robin Najar
Production: Sonja S. Chapman
Typesetter: Eric Rosenbloom, Kirby Mountain Composition
Cover design: Lisa A. Fowler
Manufacturing: Steve Bernier

Printed in the United States of America on acid-free paper
13 12 11 10 09   VP   1 2 3 4 5

Contents

The Approach: Guiding student learning in a nonthreatening manner to help students understand without necessarily accepting evolution

Evolution Is Essential: Helping students recognize that evolution is one of the most powerful ideas in science, and that they need to understand it to make sense of practical issues in everyday living

Religion Is Valuable: Teaching not to undermine students' beliefs, but to make sure they are understanding this key concept

Teaching via Inquiry: Engaging students through an inquiry-based model that allows them to ask questions and to reason answers on their own

Summary

The Big Ideas and the Central Concepts: Deciding the focus of your unit so that students remember the big ideas

The Essential Question: Choosing an inspiring question leading to conversation, exploration, and application

Summary

CHAPTER THREE: ENGAGING STUDENTS IN STUDYING EVOLUTION ■ 27

Understanding Engagement in Inquiry: Engaging students effectively in the study of evolution by tying it to scientific questions they already have about life or the world around them

Understanding Religious Conflicts: The three positions of scientism, deism, and theism, and how those positions can help you understand your students and conflicts that may arise in your classroom

Selecting an Engaging Experience: Ways to engage your students through real-life applications (for mixed classrooms) and through understanding their concerns (for classrooms with mostly resistant students)

Discussing the Experience: Guiding your students through discussions of experiences and concerns they have

Introducing the Unit Essential Question: Solidifying students' focus on the actual science involved

Dealing with Objections: Building a list of objections while laying a foundation for effectively examining them throughout the unit on evolution

Summary

CHAPTER FOUR: GUIDING STUDENTS TO EXAMINE THE EVIDENCE FOR EVOLUTION ■ 44

Selecting the Evidence for Students to Examine: Choosing resources for guided inquiry

Guiding Students to Examine the Evidence for Natural Selection: An inquiry-based lesson you can use for introducing your students to evidence for natural selection

Accommodating Resistant Students During Inquiry: Establishing an intellectually safe environment for resistant students and acknowledging their objections without losing focus on the lesson

Guiding Students to Examine the Evidence for Evolution: Continuing the plan of starting with evidence, not explanations, for introducing students to evidence for evolution itself

Summary

CHAPTER FIVE: GUIDING STUDENTS TO EXAMINE EVOLUTION ITSELF ■ 59

Natural and Supernatural Explanations: Helping your students understand the difference between natural and supernatural explanations and how the scientific worldview does not allow supernatural explanations

The Lessons: Three sample lessons that focus on explanations of evidence and help students better understand the theory of evolution itself

Explaining Whale Evolution: Extending the lesson on evidence of whale evolution to an understanding of the logic of scientists' arguments for whales' evolving from terrestrial mammals

Explaining Antiviral Resistance: Focusing students on their understanding of the theory of evolution itself within the context of a lesson on antibiotic-resistant HIV strains

Explaining Bird Evolution: A variety of instructional methods to keep students focused on developing a general understanding of evolution

Summary

CHAPTER SIX: DEEPENING STUDENTS' UNDERSTANDING AND ADDRESSING OBJECTIONS ■ 76

Scientific Worldview: Guiding students, through inquiry, to understand the nature of scientific explanations

Objections to Evolution: Addressing students' objections by helping them build the scientific understandings they'll need

Objections About Deep Time: Ways to develop lessons addressing students' objections rooted in young-Earth views.

Objections Based on Misunderstandings of Evolution Itself: Ways to develop lessons addressing objections grounded in misconceptions about the theory itself

Objections Based on Beliefs: Minilessons for addressing religious objections to evolution

Other Objections: Minilessons for addressing other objections to evolution

Summary

Acknowledgments

I admire the humility Sir Isaac Newton expressed when he said, "If I have seen a little further it is by standing on the shoulders of Giants." If I am seeing something new and insightful in the teaching of evolution, then it's only because of all of the teachers, professors, colleagues, and friends who have boosted me up to help me get a new view. A few I can name here, but the list of those shoulders upon which I stand is truly too long to write down.

I would have never talked or written about teaching evolution to resistant students without the encouragement and insight of David Jackson of the University of Georgia. He got me thinking about understanding, not believing, as the proper goal of evolution education. I would have never written this book without Emily Birch, my editor at Heinemann, who believed in the project even before I did. She encouraged me throughout the writing and gave me wise guidance. I would have also given up on the whole idea of trying to understand evolution at all, much less write about teaching it, without the constant support of my wife, Beth. She believes in my big dreams every day.

Robin Najar, Sonja Chapman, and the rest of the team at Heinemann skillfully guided me through the writing and publication process; I couldn't ask for better support. Lincoln Clark at Berry Middle School invited me into his class of amazing middle schoolers, and I walked out realizing how much I knew about teaching students of this wonderful age. Rob Angus, my colleague at the University of Alabama at Birmingham, put *Evolutionary Analysis* (Freeman and Herron 2004) in my hand and unknowingly gave me a big boost in understanding the evidence for evolution. Josh Hubbard, Chris Morrow, Jason Noah, and Jeff Rozelle blogged with me as I wrote and gave me valuable insight and encouragement. Mike Blackburn, Gordon Bals, Jeremy Carter, Jason Johnson, Kathryn Roach, and Laura Thornburg helped my family find our way through the storm that blew on us as I was writing, and my sons, David and Ben, let me lean on them. And Arlene Elrod invited me to see Lucy!

Introduction

I had just landed in Houston and was heading to my hotel when my cell phone rang. The call was from my friend Arlene: "Lee, I got us all VIP tickets to see Lucy! Want to come?" Without hesitating for even a moment, I said, "Absolutely!" As I hung up, I knew my journey to understand evolution had taken another big step forward.

Even a few years earlier, Arlene's invitation would have hit me hard. I knew immediately which Lucy she was talking about. This wasn't really a person; it was the nickname of a fossil. This was The Lucy, the fossil classified as *Australopithecus afarensis* and called "Dinkenesh" by Ethiopians. Lucy is one of the key fossils that scientists use to explain how humans and other primates evolved from a common ancestor. Lucy is clear evidence for evolution, but I wasn't scared anymore.

Years ago, I would have been intimidated by seeing Lucy. I might not have said so out loud, but inside, I would have been pretty anxious. I'm religious, and my faith is at the core of who I am and what I believe about how the world works. Back then, Lucy and much of the other scientific evidence for evolution were threats to my particular faith traditions. Like many Americans, some of your students, and maybe even you yourself, I saw conflict between my faith and science. I actually loved them both, and the conflict was truly difficult at times.

When I went to see Lucy, inside I knew I had taken a big step. I saw her bones, and I listened to the scientific explanation of how the structure of

Lucy's knee joint shows *Australopithicus afarensis* to be a transitional form between apes and humans. Rather than being afraid of the evidence for evolution, I was curious. I was even intrigued. I approached the Lucy Exhibit[1] with much more of an open mind and much less fear. I wanted to understand everything that I saw, but at the same time I didn't feel compelled to change my beliefs.

The Approach to Teaching Evolution

This book is about helping your students who are resistant to learning evolution to do so without fear, similar to how I approached seeing Lucy. It's about implementing an approach to teaching evolution in which you guide students to understand evolution but don't require that they necessarily accept it as truth. Now, you probably won't teach about Lucy and human evolution; that's much too controversial for most secondary school classrooms. But in this book, you'll find ways to guide your students to approach the study of evolution with more confidence and less fear, with a more open mind and less antagonism.

In essence, the approach in this book requires that resistant students understand evolution, but they don't necessarily have to accept it. They need to understand first the evidence for evolution. They may not accept the evidence, but they need to consider the preponderance of scientifically valid evidence. They also need to understand how scientists explain all of that evidence with the theory of evolution. Students don't have to accept evolution, even after the unit is over, but they do need to understand that evolution is a powerful and reasonable scientific explanation, and as such, it sticks to the rules of science, which disallow supernatural explanation. Resistant students therefore also need to understand the difference between natural and supernatural explanations. This distinction is key to this approach to teaching evolution. Students need to understand that science limits explanations to those resulting from natural causes, but

---

[1]www.lucyexhibition.com.

students can continue to believe that the supernatural exists and was involved in the development of life on Earth. Understanding the evidence for evolution and how scientists explain that evidence is the goal for all students, including students who resist learning about evolution. They don't have to accept evolution to understand it, however.

From the start, please don't think that this is a creationist book or one advocating the teaching of intelligent design. Both creationism and intelligent design invoke supernatural explanations of scientific evidence, and both are therefore incorrect approaches in public schools. Again and again, major scientific organizations and American courts have said that neither creationism nor intelligent design is appropriate for the public school classroom. They're also incorrect approaches to science itself. The strength of science is that it limits itself to natural explanations. I'm concerned that invoking supernatural explanations leads to confusion, especially because the scientific community would have to decide which religions provide the best supernatural explanations. I'm also concerned that students ever think that creationism and intelligent design have validity among scientists. I was myself a student resistant to learning about evolution, and I made it through my junior and senior high school science classes still believing that creationism was valid scientifically. I didn't know what to do when my college biology teacher refused to discuss creationism with me. I don't want other resistant students to be shocked, as I was, by the stark reality that neither creationism nor intelligent design has credence among the scientific community.

Also, from the start, please don't think that this book's approach to teaching evolution will undermine students' faith. A small, vocal group of scientists use science to decry religion, and I've seen some science teachers, possibly well intentioned, who advocate using the teaching of evolution to undermine children's beliefs. That's totally inappropriate for public school teachers! From my view, science teachers trying to drive out students' beliefs is just as inappropriate as teaching creationism or intelligent design. This is true whether that intention is overt or subtle. Public schools must embrace diversity of all kinds, including students from all religious backgrounds. Public schools must not establish religion, but they must not undermine it.

Book Overview

Table I.1 gives an overview of the contents of this book, framed according to questions that teachers often ask about how to teach evolution to resistant students. As you examine the table, note that I've taken an inquiry-based approach to the teaching of the evolution unit. For the last several years, I've been learning about inquiry, how to use it in my own practice, and how to help science teachers better implement inquiry in their teaching (Eick, Meadows, and Balkcom 2005; Meadows 2008); so, when approaching the teaching of any science topic, including evolution, my first tendency is to approach it via inquiry.

More important, though, the nature of inquiry lends itself to reducing the conflict resistant students perceive regarding learning about evolution. This is because inquiry, at its very core, is a cycle of evidence and explanation (Meadows 2007). Inquiry asks students to learn the ideas of science by first looking at evidence and then trying to explain that evidence in a way that matches accepted science. Unlike traditional instruction, which often asks students to accept the ideas of science simply because the teacher or book says so, inquiry directs students to understand that all scientific ideas must develop from trustworthy evidence. If you teach your evolution unit via inquiry, therefore, you won't be asking your students to accept evolution just because you say so. Instead, through inquiry, you guide students to see for themselves how evolution explains well a vast amount of scientific evidence. Inquiry then becomes the missing link in the controversy about teaching evolution because it links resistant students with the scientific evidence and explanations in the least threatening way.

To illustrate this approach to teaching evolution, you'll find outlines of lessons plans in many of the chapters. These plans show you how I envision inquiry being used and how to accommodate the needs of resistant students during the lessons. The lesson plans are detailed outlines, but many of them are not yet ready to teach. You need to create resources for your students to use in some of the lessons, filling in the lesson outline based on the specific needs and interests of your students. I've also not attempted to provide you with a complete unit of lesson plans, instead

Table I.1   Chapter Topics and Key Questions Addressed

Chapter	Topic	Questions Addressed
1	Framing the Issues	What do you mean by teaching so that students understand, but don't accept, evolution? Why can't I just skip evolution and focus on teaching other important science? Why can't I just ignore my resistant students' conflicts with evolution? What is inquiry? Isn't it chaotic and frustrating?
2	Deciding the Focus of Your Unit	What science content should my unit focus on? What resources can I tap to help me decide what to include and what to leave out? How can I shape the central focus of my unit into an essential question to guide student learning?
3	Engaging Students in Studying Evolution	How can the first essential feature of inquiry help me kick off the unit well without alienating resistant students from the start? Do I have to understand all my students' different beliefs in order to teach resistant students effectively?
4	Guiding Students to Examine the Evidence for Evolution	How does the second essential feature of inquiry help me reduce conflict by first focusing students on evidence? Which evidence should I guide my students to examine? What resources can I tap? How do I accommodate the needs of my resistant students as we look at the evidence for evolution?
5	Guiding Students to Examine Evolution Itself	What is the difference between natural and supernatural explanations? Why does science not allow supernatural explanations? How does the evolution of whales, HIV, and birds help students understand the basics of evolutionary theory?
6	Deepening Students' Understanding and Addressing Objections	How does the study of evolution help students better understand the scientific worldview? How does understanding the scientific worldview help resistant students engage in learning about evolution? How do I address students' objections about evolution?
7	Using Project-Based Learning to Solidify Student Understanding	How does project-based learning support inquiry-based learning? How can I provide multiple project options to meet the diverse needs of *all* my students? What are some possible projects I could use?
8	Wrapping Up	What are the big ideas I should remember about teaching evolution to resistant students? How do I respond when my students ask, "What do you believe?"
Appendix	Help! I'm a Biology Teacher, and I Don't Think I Understand Evolution Myself!	I've always had my own doubts about evolution. What evidence can I look at to help me understand it better? I'm new to science teaching, and I've not really studied evolution much at all. What resources will help me get my content knowledge up to speed? How can understanding whale evolution, radiometric dating, and human evolution help me deepen my understanding of evolution?

giving you only lessons key to covering the basic concepts of evolution. You need to create additional lessons addressing requirements of your curriculum that I couldn't anticipate or other aspects of your unique situation, such as prior knowledge your students may lack.

If your own study of evolution has been tentative or if you're coming to this book as a teacher new to the teaching of evolution, you might start first by reading the Appendix. I wrote it specifically for teachers who, for various reasons, feel that they need to strengthen their content knowledge about evolution. In the Appendix, I point you to many Web-based resources that you can tap to build your understanding of evolution. In fact, throughout the whole book, you'll find frequent references to free, online resources that should help you with planning and implementing a quality evolution unit.

If you're an experienced teacher of evolution, I hope you step back a little, ponder your practice, and find ways to help your students learn better. If you've been teaching using mostly traditional approaches, then the descriptions of inquiry-based lessons will help you think about alternative ways you could guide student learning about evolution. If you have taught evolution to resistant students before, the accommodations for resistant students should give you new ways to approach the controversy. A key difference between this approach and more traditional approaches is that it doesn't ask you to get involved in helping students resolve conflicts between their understanding of science and their beliefs.

Of course, regardless of your background or experience, modify and tweak what you read here. Use these ideas as a springboard for finding your own successful strategies. If you teach in a setting for which inquiry is inappropriate or difficult, you can convert these student-centered inquiries into ones that are teacher led. If you're unsure about the accommodations for resistant students, you could try a few lessons in your unit rather than throughout the whole unit, as I advocate. If those few lessons work, you can add more in the future when you teach evolution again. You're the one who knows your students and their needs the best. My main hope is that this book helps you find new ways to teach evolution well as you nurture the growth of all your students, including those who are resistant.

Three Clarifications

I've talked only about teaching resistant students thus far, but I will by no means leave out your students who are open to learning evolution. In fact, as you read, you'll see that my focus is on teaching *all* students, regardless of whether they have apprehensions about learning evolution. The lesson plan outlines describe the teaching for all students, and a separate column addresses how to accommodate resistant students' needs while you are teaching the lesson. I use the same idea of accommodation that teachers already use for English language learners or exceptional education students: Each lesson plan focuses first on teaching all students, then addresses accommodating the needs of resistant students and the challenges they face within that lesson.

I use Internet resources throughout the book and a common format for referencing them. For example, one of the best site resources I found is the evolution website[2] from WGBH in Boston (Google keywords: evolution WGBH). Throughout the book, I almost always reference websites like I just did for the evolution site. I give you the actual URL in a footnote, but because those are difficult to type in correctly from a page in a book, I give you a small set of keywords that you can use in a Google search, which should pull the site up as one of the top Google hits. You can then refer to the URL given in the footnote to make sure you're going to the correct site. The only exception to this format will be if the URL is so easy that it's almost foolproof to type. For example, in the discussion of objections in Chapter 3, I refer you to the TalkOrigins.org website as I just did because its URL is so straightforward. With these simple URLs, I won't even include the "http" or "www" portions, since on most browsers you don't have to enter those to end up in the right place.

I haven't mentioned yet students who are resistant to learning evolution specifically because of their faith. As many science teachers have experienced, some students' religions can create significant barriers to their study of evolution. This is by no means true for all religions, however.

---

[2]www.pbs.org/wgbh/evolution/.

Many students see no conflict between their faith and their study of evolution. Others do see conflict, and for some of them, the conflict is deep and dramatic. In talking about religious students who are resistant to studying evolution, I've worked throughout the writing to avoid excluding any religious groups, but I've struggled to find terms that are broad enough to describe the breadth of religions present in American classrooms. In describing local religious groups, I use a term such as *faith community* rather than *church, synagogue,* or any other term specific to any one religion. I use the term *religious leader* or *spiritual mentor* rather than *pastor, mullah, priest,* or *rabbi.* I ask your patience if at times these terms seem unnecessarily vague or awkward, and I ask your understanding if my Christianity blinds me to times when I still use exclusive language. I truly want students from all backgrounds to be drawn into the study of evolution, but I'm still learning about what that means for people whose faith is different than mine.

Framing the Issues

You know the issues that your resistant students face when you start teaching evolution. You've seen them struggle. You've had a student raise his hand and say, "You mean God didn't create the world?" You could see a little bit of fear in his eyes. You've watched a bright student take her first zero ever because she wouldn't even attempt the evolution test. You were impressed with her zeal, but saddened by the impact on her academic record. You've tried patiently to answer the same objections period after period from the kids who had been given some kind of list of "Questions to Ask Your Teacher About Evolution." You could tell that they were wholeheartedly devoted to this life-or-death battle, as they had been coached. You know that for many of your students, studying evolution touches on much bigger issues than just fossils and change over time.

Each year, you may even dread the evolution unit about as much as your students do. You know how threatening it is to some students and how they brace themselves when the unit starts. They're either scared of what's coming or preparing themselves for a fight. They don't really know, though, how difficult it may be for you. If you teach middle school, you know how important it is to nurture your students through the life changes that they're facing. You know how confusing their lives can be at times. If you're a high school teacher, you know how important it is to guide your students to solidify their understandings of science. Yours could be the last biology course they ever take. For middle and high school students, evolution can actually increase the confusion and conflict in their lives, and sometimes you may wonder if teaching the topic is necessary or even appropriate.

Part of the problem you're facing is not due to evolution itself, however. It's due to the approach we take to the teaching of evolution. This chapter overviews a different approach, one that offers a method for engaging your students without threatening their worldviews. This chapter also overviews inquiry-based teaching—how it can be used as part of the approach to guide students to see scientific evidence and how this evidence has developed into the theory of evolution as a powerful, sensible explanation for how life works on Earth.

The Approach

The approach to teaching evolution in this book advises teachers to guide resistant students to understand evolution but not necessarily accept it, and you have probably never heard of this way of teaching evolution. It's something that my friend David Jackson and I started working on in the mid 1990s. For many science teachers, this approach is a new idea because they've thought that resolving the conflict was the only option.

You probably know the resolution approach, even if you've never heard that term. The resolution approach demands that beliefs about the supernatural and scientific understandings have to be resolved. The two have to square up. If scientific evidence conflicts with what religion teaches, then one of them is wrong, and we have to find out which one is in error. Both can't be true.

With the resolution approach in the science classroom, however, scientific evidence has the upper hand, and pretty much everyone knows it. Teachers know that their duty is to teach evolution. It's in the textbooks and the curriculum documents. It's a central idea of science. Students also usually figure out that science has the trump card in the science class. They may come in defensive and they may argue, but they almost always find out that they're not going to change their teacher's mind. They then might continue to fight, but mainly for their dignity and not really to defeat evolution.

In the American science classroom, resolution is usually implemented in one of two fashions. It's either "Check your beliefs at the door" or "Evolution? What evolution?" In the first strategy, teachers focus only on the science side of the controversy, and they don't address other worldview issues at all. They may do this blatantly by saying something like, "This is a science class, not Sunday school. We're not going to discuss religion." They may do it more subtly by simply sidestepping resistant students' concerns or suggesting that the students talk to someone else who can advise them on spiritual matters. This approach to resolution honors the science but ignores students' humanity and how they are trying to make sense of science in the broad worldview context of their beliefs about God, life, and how the world works.

In the second resolution approach, teachers simply leave evolution out. Either they don't teach it at all or they cover it really quickly just to meet the expectations of their curriculum or administration. Their goal is to not upset their students or offend spiritual leaders in their communities. For example, teachers may teach only natural selection. They cover how species change over time in adaptation to their environment, but they don't teach the scientific evidence for the origin of new species or for the evolution of life itself on Earth. This approach honors students' beliefs, but it cheats them of a deep understanding of science, including the brilliance of evolutionary theory and its explanatory power in every living system we encounter.

This book presents a third approach to the conflict. It's a different way than the dead-end street of resolution. It's in the category of what personal leadership guru Steven Covey (1989) calls a "third alternative" (271). He wisely points out that often when humans are in conflict, we usually see only two ways: my way or your way. If the two ways are incompatible, then we're at a dead end unless one of us gives up. Covey points out that in those dead-end conflicts, we have to look for a third alternative, a new way that neither of us has thought of before, one in which we both win. This is Covey's "win/win" agreement, a term you've probably heard of. This third approach to teaching evolution can be that win/win.

In this approach, teachers open up the classroom by allowing students to examine the scientific evidence for evolution and how scientists explain that evidence, but teachers don't expect students to fully accept either. Some highly resistant students might not accept any of the evidence or explanation covered, some may accept portions only, but all students will at least understand. As the rest of this books shows, during the evolution unit, students consistently hear their teachers say, "I expect you to understand _____, but I don't expect you necessarily to accept it," where the blank is filled in with essential science content about evolution. In this approach, teachers affirm the value and beauty of students' beliefs while also guiding them to examine the evidence for evolution and its place as a powerful explanation of science. Teachers support students in the hard intellectual work of encountering the support for and implications of evolutionary theory, but teachers also recognize that for many students, this can be highly threatening, and teachers don't seek to overturn students' worldviews.

Evolution Is Essential

The approach I advocate doesn't undermine evolution as a powerful idea of science. Evolution is a cornerstone of science, one of the most powerful ideas in all of science. Theodosius Dobzhansky (1973) said, "Nothing in biology makes sense except in the light of evolution" (125). If students don't understand evolution, they really don't understand biology.

Without an understanding of evolution, students will have a hard time making sense of many practical issues they will face in life. Think about vaccinations for viruses. Evolution explains why some viral diseases can be controlled by vaccines and others can't. For example, smallpox has been eradicated by a single vaccine, but flu vaccines must be reformulated each year. Evolution explains the difference. Viral genes control the virus surface structures that our immune systems respond to in fighting off viruses. In smallpoxe these genes don't evolve, but in the flu these genes evolve slowly. Scientists develop a vaccine for the flu one year, but then the virus changes and that vaccine is no longer effective. This is why developing a vaccine for HIV is so difficult. Surface structure genes in HIV evolve rapidly even during a single infection. All students, including students who don't believe in evolution, need to understand evolution in order to make good decisions about keeping themselves healthy.

Consider also how evolution provides a powerful explanation about DNA and transmission of genetic information. Taxonomic trees were constructed previously based on form and function. Now, though, DNA provides compelling evidence about which species are most closely related by analyzing the similarities in their genetic structures. Evolution provides a clear explanation of this DNA evidence. Common ancestors would have passed on their DNA to their descendents, but changes in the DNA resulted in differences in the subsequent generations of their offspring. Evolution explains the DNA differences. All students need to see that evolution plays a central role in biological explanations, even if they don't believe that life on Earth evolved without supernatural intervention.

The centrality of evolution in biology is subtle, but far-reaching; the doors to science may be shut in front of students of faith if they don't learn evolution. Students who continue their science studies in college biology will encounter the clear consensus in the scientific community that evolution is a fact. They will hear almost every college biology professor state that life occurred by evolution. No credence is given to special creation or intelligent design. Although many biologists are people of faith, in their classrooms and in their work, they go about their day with evolution as the only credible theory. There is no other scientific explanation! Science-oriented students of faith will face serious challenges if they can't work from an understanding of evolution, leaving their beliefs to after-hours discussions. This situation is made much more difficult if secondary science teachers give credence to creationist theories in their classrooms. They're actually making things worse, not better, for resistant students who pursue science studies in college.

This isn't a problem that affects only college-bound students heading into careers as biologists. As the U.S. workforce shifts from low-skills to high-tech, more and more jobs will require scientific understandings. Students literally can't afford to cut themselves out of science-related careers because they're fearful of or turned off by evolution. They need to be comfortable with science and fluent with the understanding of the world it provides, both as people making sense of their world and as workers trying to stay competitive in a rapidly changing global economy.

Religion Is Valuable

The approach used in this book requires students to understand evolution as a bedrock conclusion of science; at the same time, it also requires teachers to honor their students' beliefs. For many students, religion brings deep meaning to life. Their spirituality is at the core of who they are. It impacts how they see the natural world, it is a key component of their identity as people, and it is central to their family and the communities in which they live.

Religion is not something to be stamped out of the science classroom, but that is what the resolution approach often communicates to children. When children hear their teacher say, "We're not going to talk about faith; we're going to stick to the science," they often hear that teacher saying, "Your faith is not important." That may be the furthest thing from their teacher's mind, but secondary school students are sensitive to rejection, and it will be hard for them not to feel that their faith is rejected if their teachers refuse to acknowledge that for many people evolution and religion intertwine.

That intertwining is especially important for science-oriented students of faith. For many of them, faith and science are mixed together in their minds and help them understand and appreciate the natural world. They see the world as a result of a creator, and they see the intricate beauty revealed by science as an expression of supernatural work. They may see their god at work in the natural world, maintaining beauty and order through natural means from weather systems to DNA replication. Their spiritual leaders may have taught them that they have a responsibility for stewarding the world, protecting it from damage and increasing its beauty, and students may see that science gives them understanding to carry out that mission. To be told in science class that they must divorce their faith from science creates a dichotomy in their mind and undermines a unity between the two that can help them makes sense of the world.

Public school teachers should never undermine their students' beliefs. Public schools cannot establish religion, but they should do no harm to it either. Teachers serve the public, and this includes serving the religious public. Parents who raise their children in faith and send them to public schools demand that those schools do no harm to their children's faith.

Many parents choose to send their children to public schools, rather than to religious schools, because they want their children to encounter different ideas than those of their own faith. Many parents value that challenge, because they want their children to learn to work out their faith in a secular world. However, they also take seriously their responsibility to protect their children from attacks on their faith that their children may not yet be ready to handle, including teachers who use their positions to undermine students' faith. Children are vulnerable. Many have not developed a full understanding of the faith in which they are being raised. Undermining students' faith is inappropriate for public school teachers: It erodes the trust between public schools and the communities they serve, and it sends the message that the teacher knows more than parents about how to raise the children involved.

Faith is also valuable to students as it informs them about the afterlife. Many students find comfort from their faith as they think about what happens to them and people they love after they die. Regardless of what a teacher may or may not believe, when teachers allow the study of evolution to undermine students' faith, they may be shaking their students' worldviews to the core. Many religious fundamentalists have been taught that they are preparing themselves in this life for either heaven or hell. The stakes are that high! They believe that their faith shows them how to escape eternal punishment. If you put yourselves in these students' shoes, it makes sense that they may resist learning about evolution if it might threaten their eternal souls. In their minds, not doing well on the evolution test and enduring the disapproval of their teacher is a small price to pay in comparison with gaining eternal paradise.

Teaching via Inquiry

The rest of this book walks you through the how-tos of the approach. The book provides concrete tools and strategies so that you can engage students in studying about evolution without threatening their faith. You'll see how to plan specific lessons and the whole evolution unit. We need to look first at inquiry, however, before we go further. Inquiry will be the context in which you guide students to understand, but not necessarily accept, evolution.

We could look at inquiry in a lot of different ways, but the most productive way I've found is with the five essential features of inquiry from the book *Inquiry and the National Science Education Standards*[1] (National Research Council 2000). The five essential features define what inquiry is and provide a framework for thinking about how inquiry is implemented in the classroom. The five essential features of inquiry follow. Take a few moments to read through the essential features and think about how you could teach a unit on evolution using an inquiry-based approach.

The Five Essential Features of Inquiry

1. Learners are engaged by scientifically oriented questions.
2. Learners give priority to evidence, which allows them to develop and evaluate explanations that address scientifically oriented questions.
3. Learners formulate explanations from evidence to address scientifically oriented questions.
4. Learners evaluate their explanations in light of alternative explanations, particularly those reflecting scientific understanding.
5. Learners communicate and justify their proposed explanations.

(from *Inquiry and the National Science Education Standards*, 24–27)

The key to using inquiry is the cycle of evidence and explanation set up by the five essential features. Notice how prominently evidence figures in inquiry. After the teacher raises a question, students first encounter evidence that they will use in answering the question. Students also use evidence as the basis for evaluating any explanations proposed as an answer to the question. In an evolution unit, evidence must be central to almost every lesson. Consider, for example, the big scientific idea that the fossil record shows millions of years of evidence of species changing over time. Is this something that you simply tell your students or something that you show them based on scientific evidence? Species change over time is a powerful

---

[1]This book is available free online from the National Academy Press. Go to books.nap.edu or Google "inquiry NSES."

scientific explanation (essential feature #3), but it's an explanation that has been developed from evidence. It only holds scientific validity if it is the best explanation of actual evidence.

Think about how much of your teaching on evolution includes actual scientific evidence. How often do you have students consider scientific data rather than expecting them simply to accept what you say when you describe how evolution happened? If you don't have them consistently consider evidence, you may be asking them to take evolution as a matter of faith, to trust you that it occurred rather than coming to their own conclusions about the power of evolution to explain scientific evidence. Can you see why some of your students of faith may get confused? They're not sure whose opinions to believe, yours or those of their spiritual leaders who taught them that their god created the world.

Note also the first word in essential feature #3 so that you see who is formulating the explanation from evidence. *Learners*—students, not teachers—should make sense of the data in order to answer scientific questions. Using inquiry doesn't mean that the teacher isn't involved, but it does mean that students have to shoulder the responsibility of making sense of the data. They have to put their heads as wells as hands on the evidence and think through its implications. Much of the time, they'll need help from teachers in the form of structured guidance that they follow for developing their explanations. Teachers can scaffold the process for students through tools such as small-group discussions, graphic organizers, or tables and charts, as you'll see in later chapters of this book. Through the inquiry process, students learn that scientific explanations must develop from scientific evidence, and this understanding is critical for all students, even resistant ones, if they are going to understand evolution as an explanation for data from the natural world.

I don't advocate an open-ended inquiry approach to teaching evolution, however. Instead, I focus on guided inquiry. Almost every teacher I've ever worked with is skeptical of students choosing their own questions, making up their own procedures and methods of analysis, guiding themselves through data collection and analysis, and developing their own write-ups. Students might do one of these things at certain times, but doing them all within the same inquiry leads to frustration and chaos. Open inquiry does have value for helping students learn how to identify and attack questions through scientific methods, but it takes a lot of time for students to develop the high-level skills they need to be successful in open inquiry. With evolution especially, an open-ended approach could be a total dead end since the questions involved are so big.

This distinction between open and guided inquiry is critical. Take a look at Table 1.1, which should further clarify the differences between the two approaches. In Table 1.1, the Open Inquiry column gives examples of things a teacher using an open approach might say. On first read, some teacher statements in that column may sound good, but I can't imagine regular secondary students having much success if this all they hear from their teacher before they begin work. Now, look at the Guided Inquiry column; guided inquiry leads to more success in the typical classroom. Guidance allows students to be successful in each phase of the inquiry, and the inquiry itself keeps students both active and engaged in seeing how evolution is a logical explanation for actual evidence.

Table 1.1   Open Inquiry Compared with Guided Inquiry

Essential Feature	Open Inquiry	Guided Inquiry
1. Learners are engaged by scientifically oriented questions.	"I want you to think of a question you'd like to explore about animal survival."	"Over the next week, we'll be thinking about the question, How do organisms adapt to their environment?"
2. Learners give priority to evidence . . .	"I want each group to develop and implement an experiment you could conduct to answer the question you came up with."	"Take a look at the instructions for today's lab on bacterial adaptation. With your group, review the six steps now and prepare yourselves to ask any questions about what you'll be doing in lab."
3. Learners formulate explanations . . .	"Work with your group to develop an explanation for the data you collected."	"With your group, make a bar graph of the insect data from 1965, 1985, and 2005. Then, prepare a summary statement of which species appear to be diminishing and which appear to be increasing."
4. Learners evaluate their explanations . . .	"Check your explanation. You might want to use the Internet or the text. You even could call a scientist. Just make sure you're on the right track."	"Read pages 175–177 of your textbook. Then, read Dr. Joyce Smith's explanation, as it appears on her website. Compare your explanations with the book's and Dr. Smith's. Make adjustments to your explanation if you think you need to in order to better explain the evidence you collected."
5. Learners communicate and justify their proposed explanations.	"Write up your inquiry. Make sure you cover everything important and that it's clearly written."	"Make a pamphlet that would help fourth and fifth graders understand the fossil record and why it's important. Include actual scientific evidence in your pamphlet so that your audience knows that your explanations are scientific and not simply opinions."

Summary

Resolving the evolution conflict is a dead-end street. When science teachers focus on the resolution between religion and evolution, they create an insurmountable tension for many students of faith. Students are put in the position where they have to decide which is right—science or faith. The resolution approach creates a false dichotomy, forcing students to make a choice when no choice is actually necessary. Students can learn and understand how evolution explains the vast amounts of scientific evidence without feeling that they necessarily have to accept that evolution happened.

An inquiry-based approach to teaching evolution allows students to hold onto their beliefs while they are moving toward more scientific understandings of the history of life on Earth and how evolution functions today. Teachers who use this approach do not threaten or attack students' beliefs because students build their understanding of evolution based on scientific evidence and explanations, rather than basing it on the authority of the teacher or the textbook. Teachers guide students to see evolution as a powerful explanation for the scientific evidence they examine, but teachers don't rush the students toward some final synthesis of their scientific and spiritual worldview, recognizing that positive experience studying evolution now lays a good foundation for openness to learning about evolution in the future.

As you can imagine, teaching by inquiry and with a goal of understanding, but not necessarily accepting, evolution takes skill and planning. Consider what you hope to accomplish during the unit, the scientific evidence you'll have your students examine, and how you'll guide students to understand the explanations scientists have developed for that evidence. Investing some time in planning before you actually jump into teaching will help you engage your students in learning about evolution without feeling like their beliefs are under attack.

Deciding the Focus
of Your Unit

Teaching your unit on evolution in a way that doesn't threaten students' beliefs requires careful planning. You have a lot to consider as you prepare the unit: the objections your students may raise; how much they already know about evolution; your goal for the unit, including deciding which scientific understandings aren't developmentally appropriate for your students. You'll also begin gathering resources that you can tap for deepening your understanding of evolution and how to teach it in such a way that all students are engaged in learning.

First, think about the goal of the unit, including the central concepts you're going to target and the essential question you'll use to guide your teaching and your students' learning. Consider your students' prior understandings as they come into the unit. What do they know already about evolution, and what misunderstandings might they have? Also, what do they know about the nature of science, and how might they be confused about how science works? Plan for the actual evidence you'll have your students encounter, selecting from the vast amount of evidence what will be most meaningful and productive for your students in building their understanding of evolution. Gather resources that you'll use for teaching the unit, including those that help you better understand evolution itself and how to teach it to your students. This chapter walks you through these issues so that when you begin teaching, you are confident that you're teaching important scientific ideas in a meaningful, respectful way for your students.

The Big Ideas and the Central Concepts

You're probably familiar with the current move in education toward teaching big ideas and concepts. Grant Wiggins and Jay McTighe (2005) have called for this kind of teaching, and they've outlined a process for finding it called "Backward Design." Bernice McCarthy's (2000) theory of natural learning, the 4MAT system, centers every instructional unit on a central concept that teachers return to again and again throughout the unit. In science, this move is seen in the less-is-more approach advocated by Project 2061 and Science for All Americans (Rutherford and Ahlgren 1990). Mastering the big ideas of science results in students' achieving science literacy, which is a central theme of the National Science Education Standards (National Research Council 1996).

Why a Conceptual Approach?

Students forget the facts. Actually, we all do. When I taught chemistry for several years, I had all the facts about the first thirty or so elements in the periodic chart memorized cold, including atomic masses down to three or four decimal places. My students were amazed! They'd ask, "How do you know all that without looking?" What amazed me, though, was when I went back to teaching chemistry after three years out of the classroom, almost all of those facts had disappeared from my memory! I really thought the facts would be there for life. If we as teachers forget the facts when we know them more deeply than most of our students ever will, then we have to assume that our students will forget the facts as well. So, what should we focus on?

Big ideas, major understandings, and large concepts stick with us for a lifetime. I may have forgotten the atomic mass of sulfur, but I still to this day know what atomic mass is, why it's an important scientific idea, and how it is catalogued clearly in periodic charts. The big ideas of science should be our focus, and evolution is one of the truly big ideas of science. Others include such major understandings as plate tectonics; the position of the Earth in the solar system, our galaxy, and the universe; atomic structure and molecular motion; Newton's laws of motion; and the cell as the fundamental unit of most living organisms (Rutherford and Ahlgren 1990).

Using inquiry, each investigation you plan should further unfold the evolution unit's central concept or cluster of concepts. It's as if the central concept were a masterpiece statue in the center of a room of a museum. Looking at the statue quickly and from one angle only isn't enough. Deep understanding takes multiple views, from multiple perspectives. That's what you're doing with the concept of evolution in this unit: You're walking students around the statue and helping them see from multiple views why scientists consider evolution a masterpiece of scientific thinking.

The Big Idea

What do you want your students to remember after they've forgotten all the facts? If you teach middle school, what do you want your students to take with them into their study of biology in high school? If you teach high school biology, what do you want your students to remember for life, especially those students who won't study biology again? Most facts will be long gone from their memories even just a few months after their studies end. They probably won't remember the difference between *hominids* and *hominins*, but you hope they will remember how scientists developed the explanation of descent from a common ancestor to explain the wealth of fossil evidence across multiple continents and millions of years of fossil evidence. When your students are adults, how do you want them to be able to use their understanding of evolution in their daily lives? By then, they'll have forgotten which species you chose as an example to help them understand natural selection, but they will need to apply an understanding of natural selection as they think about how the human impact on our environment gives some species an evolutionary advantage and drives other species toward extinction.

These kinds of questions cause us to look for a big idea that is important and memorable. The best resource I've found for helping me find those big ideas is Project 2061's *Atlas of Science Literacy* (2001). Before I found *Atlas*, I spent hours, maybe even days or weeks, deciding how to focus my teaching. Now, I've realized that *Atlas* does almost all of that work for me. The big ideas and why they are important are clearly there for quick reference. The only disadvantage of *Atlas* is that it's not available online. You can see sample maps at Project 2061's website (project2061.org), but to see all of the maps, including the maps most helpful for planning your evolution unit, you'll have to buy a copy of *Atlas.* So, in this book I'll refer instead to the conceptual building blocks of the *Atlas* maps, which are from Project 2061's *Benchmarks for Science Literacy* (American Association for the Advancement of Science 1993).

Benchmarks for Science Literacy states what students should know and be able to do regarding each big idea of science at four grade levels: after second grade (primary science), after fifth grade (at the end of elementary school), after eighth grade (as they move from middle to high school), and by graduation from high school. The benchmarks help you see where science learning should be focused at your level of teaching. For middle school teachers, the elementary benchmarks help you see what students should know from their previous studies of science, and the high school benchmarks help you see what they should study later on. The high school benchmarks also help middle-level teachers see what they can hold off on teaching, especially since these concepts are probably developmentally inappropriate for middle school students. For high school teachers, the elementary and middle-level benchmarks describe the prior knowledge your students should have as they begin their study of evolution with you. In the tables throughout this chapter, you'll see my compilation of ideas from *Atlas* and *Benchmarks* to help you find a focus for the evolution unit.

Let's first start with the long-term view of what your students should remember when their formal school experiences are over. What do they need to know for everyday life as adults, especially if they don't work in science or science-related careers? Here, an *Atlas* map is actually available online that can help answer that question. Please take the time to find the "Explaining Evolution" *Atlas* map[1] at Project2061.org (Google keywords: explaining evolution atlas). This map calls for a deep understanding of evolution. It's not enough for students just to memorize facts; they need to see how the ideas connect together into a single big idea, a large conceptual understanding of evolution. This depth of knowledge requires understandings from geology and understandings about the nature of science itself, which may not be possible even after the first high school biology course.

---

[1]www.project2061.org/publications/atlas/sample/a2ch10.pdf.

Still, the map is helpful for thinking about the eventual understanding that we hope our students reach. According to Project 2061, the understandings on the Explaining Evolution map are essential for students to be considered "science literate" regarding evolution.

In the off-line portions of *Atlas*, this large understanding of evolution is broken down into two main scientific ideas—biological evolution and natural selection—that students need to know. *Atlas* includes a separate map for each idea. I suggest that your unit focus on the big ideas of evolution and natural selection, but I also suggest a third big idea for you to consider in your planning: your evolution unit should further your students' understandings of the worldview science gives us, because this is where I see many resistant students struggling to understand evolution. It's really not that evolution is the problem; instead, the problem is often that they don't understand science itself.

Let's start with worldview considerations, and then we'll loop back to evolution and see how the two mesh together. Table 2.1 helps you see how your students' learning during the evolution unit can build their understanding of the bigger issues of science, including many of the issues that can cause conflict for resistant students. Take a look at the middle-level target benchmarks in the Limits of Science column and think about your students' objections. How many students think that science tells them that their religion is wrong? Perhaps they don't understand that science is limited, that "some matters cannot be examined usefully in a scientific way" (American Association for the Advancement of Science 1993, 1A/M4ab*[2]). Science can't and shouldn't talk about whether God created the Earth. Science is limited to natural, not supernatural explanations, and any scientist who uses the evidence from evolution to argue against or for religion has stepped outside the limits of science. Note too from Table 2.1 that middle

---

[2]Throughout, this type of code indicates the location of quoted text in the online version of Benchmarks for Science Literacy. The first number indicates the chapter; in this case, Chapter 1. The next letter indicates the chapter section; in this case, Section A. The "M" indicates grade levels 6–8 ("H" is used for high school grades). The remaining portion of the code identifies the specific benchmark appearing in the corresponding section; in this case, it is the fourth of six benchmarks.

Table 2.1   Scientific Worldview Benchmarks

	Limits of Science	Avoiding Bias	The Scientific Community
Target benchmarks: high school general biology	Scientists often cannot bring definitive answers to matters of public debate. . . . The answer may involve the comparison of values that lie outside of science. 1C/H9**(SFAA)	The expectations, moods, and prior experiences of human beings can affect how they interpret new perceptions or ideas. People tend to ignore evidence that challenges their beliefs and to accept evidence that supports them. 6D/H2ab	The strongly held traditions of science, including its commitment to peer review and publication, serve to keep the vast majority of scientists well within the bounds of ethical professional behavior. Deliberate deceit is rare and likely to be exposed sooner or later by the scientific enterprise itself. 1C/H7
Target benchmarks: middle school life science	Some matters cannot be examined usefully in a scientific way. Among them are matters that by their nature cannot be tested against observation. 1A/M4ab*	What people expect to observe often affects what they actually do observe. Strong beliefs about what should happen in particular circumstances can prevent them from detecting other results. 1B/M3ab	Scientists' personal interests and viewpoints can influence the questions they investigate. 1C/M8**(SFAA)
Prior learning: key benchmarks from elementary school	Science is a process of trying to figure out how the world works by making careful observations and trying to make sense of those observations. 1A/E2** Sometimes scientists have different explanations for the same set of observations. That usually leads to their making more observations to resolve the differences. 1B/E3bc	The claims people make are sometimes based on how they feel about something rather than on what they observe. 9E/E2* There is a danger of choosing only the data that show what is expected by the person doing the choosing. 9D/E5c	Doing science involves many different kinds of work and engages men and women of all ages and backgrounds. 1C/E3

From "American Association for the Advancement of Science, *Benchmarks Online*," available at www.project2061.org. Reprinted with permission.

school students need to come to their evolution unit having gained in elementary school a basic understanding of scientific process and explanations. If they haven't learned those basics, they will probably struggle with how the process of scientific inquiry yields trustworthy explanations.

How many of your students make bad decisions in general because of their strong beliefs or because they're looking only at one side of an issue? For instance, the high school benchmarks for avoiding bias discuss how "people tend to ignore evidence that challenges their beliefs." I'm sure you've seen this happen in debates about evolution in your class or even among adults you know. People on both sides of the issue forget those facts that challenge their beliefs. The evolution unit should help your students grow in these areas as they learn to think about evidence in scientific ways. To achieve that high school level understanding, however, students will need the prior knowledge indicated in the bottom two rows of the Avoiding

Bias column. From elementary school, they'll need a foundation of experiences where they've seen how expectations can cause people to distort data. From middle school, they should have refined that understanding by seeing that expectations can cause scientists to totally miss important data.

As you review Table 2.1, think about the idea that science has limits, which may be the most helpful big idea for engaging your resistant students. Science can tell us about many things in the world around us, but there are also many things science can't explain. As *Benchmarks* shows, science can't establish morality. Science can't be used either to explain or to explain away supernatural events! Often, resistant students fear that science tells them that God doesn't exist or doesn't work in the world today. Science can't say that, even though some scientists do. I'll describe more in Chapter 6 how you can use the scientific worldview, especially the central concept that science has limits, to help your students solidify their understanding of evolution without threatening their beliefs.

Figure 2.1 is a planning sheet for teaching the scientific worldview. Take a look at the questions there, and note how the planning sheet guides you to apply the planning questions to different content from Table 2.1 depending on whether you're a middle or high school teacher. Make sure you're using the right set of questions for your grade level. You can use the questions to help think through exactly what it is from the scientific worldview that you want to include in your unit. As you think through the questions and begin to determine your answers, you're starting the process of planning your unit. Keep in mind that these scientific worldview ideas, though not the major focus of the evolution unit, are usually intertwined in the conflict many resistant students feel about studying evolution.

Next, you need to repeat the same examination process for the big ideas of biological evolution and natural selection. Tables 2.2 and 2.3 are laid out in the same format as Table 2.1, with Table 2.2 giving the benchmarks for evolution and Table 2.3 giving those for natural selection. These two big ideas are similar, and the actual *Atlas* maps show lots of connections and overlaps between the two ideas. Note that, unlike the ideas in Table 2.1, at the high school level, the two columns merge into one. This is also clear on the actual *Atlas* maps, which have lines showing the conceptual flow of ideas. For the big ideas of both evolution and natural selection, middle

Use the following questions to help you think through the concepts from Table 2.1 and decide the focus of your unit.

Questions for Examining Prior Learning: Middle school teachers should apply these questions to the Key Benchmarks from Elementary School listed in Table 2.1. High school teachers should apply the Benchmarks from Middle School Life Science listed in Table 2.1.

■ For which of these ideas do your students have solid understanding?
■ For which of these ideas do your students have tentative, or even total lack of, understanding?
■ How much time will you devote to remediating gaps in their understanding?

Questions for Examining Target Benchmarks: Apply these questions to the target benchmarks for your grade level shown in Table 2.1.

■ How do these benchmarks help you think about the goals you'll set for your students' growth during the evolution unit?
■ How can you use the idea that science has limits to ease some of your students' anxieties about evolution?
■ When your students encounter the evidence you put in front of them in the unit, how will their expectations impact how they actually see the evidence?
■ These understandings should be developed throughout the years of science instruction at your school, not just in your class or during your evolution unit. Are there benchmarks that you will depend on other teachers at your level to develop?
■ Will you try to develop your students' understanding of all of these benchmarks or are there some you will eliminate?

Questions for Examining Future Learning Goals: Middle school teachers should apply these questions to the Target Benchmarks: High School General Biology listed in Table 2.1. High school teachers should refer to *Atlas'* Explaining Evolution map.

■ How might your students struggle to understand these ideas? Which of these ideas are developmentally inappropriate for your students?
■ How does the knowledge that future teachers might develop these understandings help you decide content to eliminate?

Figure 2.1 Teaching the Scientific Worldview Benchmarks

school teachers will teach students two separate foundational ideas. High school teachers, however, will guide students to synthesize those two ideas into one big understanding. This is why the high school benchmarks in Tables 2.2 and 2.3 span both columns.

During the unit, students need to synthesize a rich, deep understanding of the major concepts given in Tables 2.2 and 2.3. Unlike the scientific worldview concepts, however, students may not encounter biological evolution during their other science studies at your school level. In other words,

Table 2.2 Biological Evolution Benchmarks

	Evidence from Existing Organisms	Fossil Evidence
Target benchmarks: high school general biology	Evolution builds on what already exists, so the more variety there is, the more there can be in the future. But evolution does not necessitate long-term progress in some set direction. 5F/H9 The basic idea of biological evolution is that the Earth's present-day species developed from earlier, distinctly different species. 5F/H1* Molecular evidence substantiates the anatomical evidence for evolution and provides additional detail about the sequence in which various lines of descent branched off from one another. 5F/H2	
Target benchmarks: middle school life science	Similarities among organisms are found in internal anatomical features and patterns of development, which can be used to infer the degree of relatedness among organisms. 5A/M3a Patterns of human development are similar to those of other vertebrates. 6B/H7	Many thousands of layers of sedimentary rock provide evidence for the long history of the Earth and for the long history of changing life forms whose remains are found in the rocks. 5F/M3a More recently deposited rock layers are more likely to contain fossils resembling existing species. 5F/M3b Sediments of sand and smaller particles (sometimes containing the remains of organisms) are gradually buried and are cemented together by dissolved minerals to form solid rock again. 4C/M3
Prior Learning: key benchmarks from elementary school	A great variety of kinds of living things can be sorted into groups in many ways using various features to decide which things belong to which group. 5A/E1	Fossils can be compared to one another and to living organisms according to their similarities and differences. Some organisms that lived long ago are similar to existing organisms, but some are quite different. 5F/E2

if their experiences during your unit don't build their understanding of these four major concepts, middle school students will probably move into their high school biology studies without the prior knowledge they need there. High school students who don't study biology again may never develop these essential understandings.

Table 2.2 notes the key concepts making up the big idea of evolution: the evidence for evolution from existing organisms and the evidence for evolution from the fossil record. The Fossil Evidence column shows that middle school students should be coming from elementary school with a basic idea of what fossils are. In middle school, students build on the understanding that the fossil record provides key evidence regarding the changes in living forms over Earth's long history. The Evidence from Existing Organisms column indicates that middle school students should have an understanding of the rich diversity of life on Earth and how life-forms can be grouped. In middle school, students need to build an understanding of how scientists use similarities among organisms to infer how closely the

Table 2.3 Natural Selection Benchmarks

	Changing Environments	**Variation and Advantage**
Target benchmarks: high school general biology	The continuing operation of natural selection on new characteristics and in changing environments, over and over again for millions of years, has produced a succession of diverse new species. 5F/H10**(SFAA) When an environment changes, including other organisms that inhabit it, the survival value of some inherited characteristics may change. 5F/H6c Natural selection leads to organisms that are well suited for survival in particular environments. 5F/H6A [Offspring of advantaged individuals] are more likely than others to survive and reproduce. As a result, the proportion of individuals that have advantageous characteristics will increase. 5F/H3* Heritable characteristics influence how likely an organism is to survive and reproduce. 5F/H4b	
Target benchmarks: middle school life science	Changes in environmental conditions can affect the survival of individual organisms and entire species. 5F/M2b	Individual organisms with certain traits are more likely than others to survive and have offspring. 5F/M2a The world contains a wide diversity of physical conditions, which creates a wide variety of environments. . . . In any particular environment, the growth and survival of organisms depend on the physical conditions. 5D/M1b*
Prior learning: key benchmarks from elementary school	Changes in an organism's habitat are sometimes beneficial to it and sometimes harmful. 5D/E4	For any particular environment, some kinds of plants and animals thrive, some do not live as well, and some do not survive at all. 5D/E1* Individuals of the same kind differ in their characteristics, and sometimes the differences give individuals an advantage in surviving and reproducing. 5F/E1

From "American Association for the Advancement of Science, *Benchmarks Online*," available at www.project2061.org. Reprinted with permission.

organisms are related to each other and that these scientific comparisons include humans. The high school benchmarks for evolution show the rich understanding students need to develop, including kinships based on DNA, the randomness of evolution, and the modern notion of the history of life on Earth from molecules to humans. Fortunately, middle school teachers don't have to tackle such big ideas.

The key concepts in Table 2.3 making up the big idea of natural selection are changing environments, or how environmental changes impact natural selection, and variety and advantage, or how evolutionary advantage occurs due to population variation. Students should come to middle school with an understanding that changes in environments can harm certain organisms and that differences among individuals of the same kind give some individuals a survival advantage. In middle school, students should expand that knowledge to an understanding that changes in the environment can affect entire species, that competition among organisms plays a key role in survival, and that specific traits are responsible for whether an individual survives and reproduces. In high school, students need to synthesize these two concepts into one big understanding of natural selection, including specifics of heredity in the process of natural selection and the understandings that variation among offspring is random and natural selection operating over millions of years is the mechanism producing the diversity of life as we see it today.

Figure 2.2 gives you some questions to think through as you step back from these standards and make some decisions about the actual content you will cover. At this point, you can make some final decisions about the actual focus of the unit. The benchmarks in Tables 2.1, 2.2, and 2.3 have helped you think through the important ideas you can focus on, but you will have to make the final decision about where to focus your instruction. Also, as noted in Figure 2.2, you need to review applicable state, district, and local standards to make sure that you're not missing required content. Hopefully, this process will give you confidence that the content you teach to your students will be valuable to them in understanding the world around them.

The Essential Question

A final, helpful step in determining the focus of a unit is deciding on an essential question to guide your and your students' focus. In the evolution unit, your students will encounter a lot of new facts and ideas, and they need help organizing those ideas so that they all fit together in a way that's meaningful (Bransford, Brown, and Cocking 1999). You can keep bringing the students back to the essential question again and again as a tool for them to make sense of everything they're studying.

Following is a long list of possible essential questions for this unit. The questions at the top of the list would be most useful for a class with only a few resistant students; the questions at the bottom would be most useful in a class where you anticipate objections from most or even all of the students. If you don't find any questions from the list that really strike you as powerful for your students, take some time and brainstorm some possible questions of your own.

Use the following questions to help you think through the concepts from Tables 2.2 and 2.3 as you decide the focus of your unit.

Questions for Examining Prior Learning: Middle school teachers should apply these questions to the key benchmarks from elementary school listed in Tables 2.2 and 2.3. High school teachers should apply the questions to the benchmarks from middle school life science.

- Which of these ideas do your students solidly understand? Which of these ideas do your students only tentatively understand, or even totally lack understanding of? How much time will you devote to remediating gaps in students' understanding?
- How do you anticipate that your resistant students may have avoided learning about evolution in previous grades, even though they may have actually been taught it? What negative experiences with evolution might you have to overcome with them before they'll ever be ready to learn about evolution with you?

Questions for Examining Target Benchmarks: Apply these questions to the target benchmarks for your grade level shown in Tables 2.2 and 2.3.

- How do these benchmarks help you decide the targets you'll set for your students' learning during the evolution unit? Will you try to develop your students' deep understanding of all of these benchmarks, or are there some you will eliminate?
- What lessons do you already have in your repertoire that you can tap for teaching these concepts?
- What missing content from your state or local curriculum guides do you also need to address?
- Have your students already mastered the target benchmarks in a previous course at your level? If so, how will you help them activate that prior learning? Are there other benchmarks that they already know?
- What are the specific conflicts that these ideas will raise with your resistant students? What about the content causes them to be anxious, fearful, or antagonistic?

Questions for Examining Future Learning Goals: Middle school teachers should apply these questions to the Target Benchmarks: High School General Biology content in Tables 2.2 and 2.3. High school teachers should apply these questions to *Atlas'* Explaining Evolution map.

- How will your students struggle to understand these ideas? Which of these ideas are developmentally inappropriate for your students?
- How does the knowledge that future teachers might develop these understandings relieve some of the weight you feel and help you to focus your unit?
- Which of these ideas have you seen turn into battles between science teachers and resistant students? Are you comfortable with simply saying something to the effect of "We're not going to study that now" if students raise questions about content that you won't cover in your course?

Figure 2.2 Teaching the Biological Evolution and Natural Selection Benchmarks

Possible Essential Questions for the Unit

Why is evolution so controversial?

Why are some people scared of evolution?

What is evolution and why should I care?

Did evolution really happen?

What's the evidence for evolution?

Are things still evolving?

Is evolution a fact?

Is evolution real?

Is evolution trustworthy?

Did we evolve?

Why should we study evolution?

Should we trust the evidence for evolution?

Are scientists who study evolution trustworthy?

Why do we have to study evolution?

Why can't we just skip evolution?

Why would anyone believe in evolution?

Can science disprove God?

In the American South, a good focus is the question "Why can't we just skip evolution?" I like it for several reasons. First, it taps into many students' feelings about evolution before instruction. Whether they're religious or not, many students know that the unit can cause big disagreements, and they'd rather just skip it. Also, the question sets up conversation about the value of studying evolution, which is something students need to understand from the unit. They shouldn't just know the facts; they should also understand why evolution is one of those big, important ideas of science for which they need to have a working understanding. I also like the way the question sets up the study of the scientific worldview benchmarks. From the first time I bring up this essential question, I've opened the door for students to talk about their understanding of how the world works. Their objections to evolution lead nicely to conversations about the limits of science and how expectations influence scientific explanations.

Summary

Now, pulling everything from this chapter together, the last two tables provide examples of the final focus for your unit. I've pulled all of the target benchmarks from Tables 2.1, 2.2, and 2.3 together in one table for each grade level, and I've eliminated the prior and future benchmarks to allow you to focus just on what the content could look like for your course. Table 2.4 gives the final focus for a middle school unit, and Table 2.5 gives the focus for a high school unit. The tables summarize the big ideas, the central concepts, and the benchmarks that become the focus of instruction for the instructional units, and these tables will be a reference point for the individual lessons discussed in future chapters.

You've probably noted that the same essential question heads both tables. Kids are kids to me, whether they're in middle or high school, and the controversy about evolution seems similar at both levels. Often, we all would just like to skip evolution and avoid the controversy; students at both levels and from all backgrounds need to find out why they really do need to study evolution.

Table 2.4   Final Unit Focus for Middle School Life Science
Essential question: "Why can't we just skip evolution?"

Big Idea	Central Concept	Target Benchmarks
Scientific worldview	Limits of science	Some matters cannot be examined usefully in a scientific way. Among them are matters that by their nature cannot be tested against observation. 1A/M4ab*
	Expectations and explanations	What people expect to observe often affects what they actually do observe. Strong beliefs about what should happen in particular circumstances can prevent them from detecting other results. 1B/M3ab
	Scientific community	Scientists' personal interests and viewpoints can influence the questions they investigate. 1C/M8**(SFAA)
Biological evolution	Evidence from existing organisms	Similarities among organisms are found in internal anatomical features and patterns of development, which can be used to infer the degree of relatedness among organisms. 5A/M3a
	Fossil evidence	Many thousands of layers of sedimentary rock provide evidence for the long history of the Earth and for the long history of changing life-forms whose remains are found in the rocks. 5F/M3a More recently deposited rock layers are more likely to contain fossils resembling existing species. 5F/M3b
Natural selection	Changing environments	Changes in environmental conditions can affect the survival of individual organisms and entire species. 5F/M2b
	Variation and advantage	Individual organisms with certain traits are more likely than others to survive and have offspring. 5F/M2a The world contains a wide diversity of physical conditions, which creates a wide variety of environments. . . . In any particular environment, the growth and survival of organisms depend on the physical conditions. 5D/M1b*

From "American Association for the Advancement of Science, *Benchmarks Online*," available at www.project2061.org. Reprinted with permission.

Table 2.5 Final Unit Focus for High School General Biology
Essential question: "Why can't we just skip evolution?"

Big Idea	Central Concept	Target Benchmarks
Scientific worldview	Limits of science	Scientists often cannot bring definitive answers to matters of public debate. . . . The answer may involve the comparison of values that lie outside of science. 1C/H9**(SFAA)
	Expectations and explanations	The expectations, moods, and prior experiences of human beings can affect how they interpret new perceptions or ideas. People tend to ignore evidence that challenges their beliefs and to accept evidence that supports them. 6D/H2ab
	Scientific community	The strongly held traditions of science, including its commitment to peer review and publication, serve to keep the vast majority of scientists well within the bounds of ethical professional behavior. Deliberate deceit is rare and likely to be exposed sooner or later by the scientific enterprise itself. 1C/H7
Biological evolution	Evidence from existing organisms and fossil evidence	Evolution builds on what already exists, so the more variety there is, the more there can be in the future. But evolution does not necessitate long-term progress in some set direction. 5F/H9
		The basic idea of biological evolution is that the Earth's present-day species developed from earlier, distinctly different species. 5F/H1*
		Molecular evidence substantiates the anatomical evidence for evolution and provides additional detail about the sequence in which various lines of descent branched off from one another. 5F/H2
Natural selection	Changing environments and variation and advantage	The continuing operation of natural selection on new characteristics and in changing environments, over and over again for millions of years, has produced a succession of diverse new species. 5F/H10**(SFAA)
		When an environment changes, including other organisms that inhabit it, the survival value of some inherited characteristics may change. 5F/H6c
		Natural selection leads to organisms that are well suited for survival in particular environments. 5F/H6A
		[Offspring of advantaged individuals] are more likely than others to survive and reproduce. As a result, the proportion of individuals that have advantageous characteristics will increase. 5F/H3*
		Heritable characteristics influence how likely an organism is to survive and reproduce. 5F/H4b

From "American Association for the Advancement of Science, *Benchmarks Online*," available at www.project2061.org. Reprinted with permission.

Now that you have a content focus for your unit, you're ready to begin planning the actual instruction you'll use to guide students to understand this content. In the next chapter, I focus on inquiry and show how you can begin the unit with the first essential feature of inquiry and engage students in the study of evolution.

Engaging Students in Studying Evolution

Whether you teach middle or high school, these students are wonderful. Middle schoolers are funny and often goofy. They are innocent and even trusting. They can be deeply insecure, but highly social at the same time. Though they're beginning some of the most significant transitions of their life, they're still boys and girls. High schoolers in ninth and tenth grade are fully into the transition to adulthood, and we can see at times the men and women that they will become. They're growing in their confidence and self-concept. They're still developing, though, still trying to make sense of their world. And now, to do your job and teach evolution, you need to engage these wonderful, insecure boys and girls or these sometimes tentative young men and women in the study of an intellectually demanding, controversial subject. You have a tough job in front of you.

A key challenge is creating a classroom environment in which each of your students feels safe to learn about evolution to the level that she or he feels comfortable. Some students from certain faith backgrounds may feel that studying about evolution is sinful. Some students may come in the door armed with pamphlets or websites and ready to do battle with you on the evils of evolution. Other students may have quietly said to themselves, "I'm just going to keep my mouth shut, spit back on the test whatever I need to know, and then forget everything I learned." They might even see the evolution unit as a chance to rebel against what their family or faith stands for. You have the complex task of drawing these students into learning, as best you can, while also meeting the needs of your students who don't object to evolution.

In this chapter, I guide you first to understand how to begin inquiry by engaging all of your students and how to understand better your resistant students in general. Then, we look at the specifics for the first two lessons you'll teach on inquiry. You'll begin the unit with an engaging experience on evolution, especially one from popular media, and then guide your students in small- and large-group discussion helping them find personal meaning in studying evolution. You'll also begin the process of better understanding your resistant students' concerns about studying evolution. You'll end the engagement portion of the inquiry by introducing the unit's essential question ("Why can't we just skip evolution?" as discussed in the previous chapter) and guiding your students to think it through for the first time.

Understanding Engagement in Inquiry

Recall from Chapter 2 that the five essential features of inquiry (National Research Council 2000) are my guide to talking about inquiry and its implementation in the classroom. Essential feature #1, the focus of this chapter, starts inquiry with getting students engaged in the scientific question they are about to examine:

> *Learners are engaged by scientifically oriented questions.* Scientifically oriented questions center on objects, organisms, and events in the natural world; they connect to the science concepts described in the content standards. They are questions that lend themselves to empirical investigation, and lead to gathering and using data to develop explanations for scientific phenomena. . . . In the classroom, a question robust and fruitful enough to drive an inquiry generates a "need to know" in students, stimulating additional questions of "how" and "why" a phenomenon occurs. . . . Fruitful inquiries evolve from questions that are meaningful and relevant to students, but they also must be able to be answered by students' observations and scientific knowledge they obtain from reliable sources. (National Research Council 2000, 24)

Please note that the question has to be both scientific and engaging for inquiry to start well. Evolution as a topic certainly passes the test of providing avenues for scientific questions; evolution is one of the foundational ideas of biology. For resistant students to study evolution via inquiry, however, teachers must also provide the kind of question that truly engages them in the subject of evolution. Look at some of the language in the earlier quote: The question needs to generate a "need to know" in your students, and it needs to be "meaningful and relevant" to your students. As you can imagine, some students do not feel that they need to know about evolution or that evolution is meaningful and relevant to their lives. They can be resistant to learning about evolution, with a stance opposite the engagement required by inquiry.

One effective way to engage students is by tying the science content to questions that they already have about life or the natural world around them. In Chapter 2, I listed possible essential questions (p. 23). Most of the engaging questions I use with students are not focused on technical science questions, such as "How does evolution explain the development of new life forms?" or "What is the difference between natural selection and evolution?" I use questions that engage all students, and I find that questions focused tightly on science content itself usually engage only the students who are naturally interested in science and willing to study it because it's intellectually satisfying to them. That's not most of the students in regular secondary school science classes, however, and we need to teach to more than 10 to 20 percent of our students. Instead, using engaging questions at the beginning of the unit can tap into questions all students have about their world. It's probably impossible to engage 100 percent of the students 100 percent of the time, but we want to begin our inquiry in such a way that as many students as possible are engaged from the start.

Don't worry about whether providing a question for students, rather than letting them generate their own, is really in keeping with inquiry. In open inquiry, students come up with their own questions. That's a difficult process for them to do well in almost any science unit, but it's particularly problematic in the evolution unit. Most students have difficulty developing a question about evolution that would be productive to guide their learning about evolution, and many resistant students are so opposed to learning about evolution that they would probably never come up with a question focused on the actual science involved. I encourage you instead to be confident that guided inquiry, in which you provide the question, is the best approach in this unit.

Understanding Religious Conflicts

Religious conflicts with evolution are deeply personal, and they will differ based on students' beliefs. The conflicts will be different among students from the Semitic religions of Christianity, Islam, or Judaism. You may have students who are from non-Semitic religions, such as Native American, Hindu, or Buddhist. You're probably also aware that the conflict can be widely different for students of the same faith. As a secondary student growing up in a fundamentalist Christian church, I approached evolution very differently than my friends who were Methodists or Episcopalians. Religious experience in America is very broad; the students in our classrooms come to the study of evolution with a wide variety of perspectives and concerns.

It would be impossible to lay out all the differences in faiths among students, especially due to their unique upbringings in the environments of your community. Instead, consider the three positions scientists themselves hold and how these positions can help you think in general about your students and how they might resist studying evolution. *Science, Evolution, and Creationism*[1] (National Academy of Sciences and Institute of Medicine 2008) describes these positions as follows:

> Scientists, like people in other professions, hold a wide range of positions about religion and the role of supernatural forces or entities in the universe. Some adhere to a position known as *scientism*, which holds that the methods of science alone are sufficient for discovering everything there is to know about the universe. Others ascribe to an idea known as *deism*, which posits that God created all things and set the universe in motion

---

[1]Available online at http://books.nap.edu (Google keywords: Science Evolution Creationism NAP).

but no longer actively directs physical phenomena. Others are *theists*, who believe that God actively intervenes in the world. (15, italics added)

This information may be a surprise to you. It was to me. I had a hunch that this was true, but I had never seen it stated so clearly by such a reputable source. This is from the National Academy of Sciences! If scientists themselves vary so much in their views about religion and supernatural intervention, we as teachers can be strongly proactive in helping our students see that they too can engage in understanding answers to scientific questions without feeling that their beliefs lock them out of the scientific community.

Some of your students may resist evolution because they come from backgrounds that lead them toward a deistic view of the world. They have been taught that a creator began everything, but doesn't intervene any more. The creator set up natural laws and processes that still are at work today, bringing order and beauty to the world. For these students, looking back along the chain of fossil evidence may bring them to a point where they experience conflict with their beliefs. You might hear some of them begin to say, "But, didn't God create everything?" The scientific explanation that life on Earth evolved by natural, not supernatural means may cause some of these students to struggle.

Theistic students will have a tougher struggle. Their faith tells them that supernatural events are still occurring around them now. They may pray, believing that their god hears their prayers and acts on their behalf. They may believe that their god still speaks to them today, either publicly in prophecy or in quieter ways when they are reading scripture or out in nature. You might hear one of them say, "But evolution just doesn't make any sense. I mean, look at all this evidence we've been studying. It's not enough. It doesn't prove anything except that God made everything the way it is now. It didn't just all magically happen on its own." Some of these students will struggle even with the limits of science itself, wanting to know why they can't use supernatural explanations to explain the evidence that you put in front of them.

This book focuses special attention on resistant theistic students[2] and

---

[2]Please note, though, that resistant theistic students typically don't believe in

their objections to evolution. Their beliefs that the supernatural is at work all around them create a basic conflict with the scientific worldview idea that events in the natural world happen because of natural, not supernatural means. The goal of this book's approach is to guide these resistant students to understand evolution well without threatening their faith. All students need to be engaged in the study of evolution, and this approach allows resistant theistic students to find a place for themselves in future science studies or even careers as they realize that they don't have to abandon their faith in order to study science. The first step of that process is engaging them in evolution at the beginning of the unit.

Selecting an Engaging Experience

Except for the few students who just really like science, I can't get my students engaged if I start with the science itself. Instead, I begin at a broader level than the content and help students understand first why studying science is important.

I describe two ways to engage your students. One is through real-life applications; the other through understanding students' concerns. The real-life application approach is designed for a classroom with a mix of students who are theistic and those who are not. The understanding concerns approach is designed for a class that is mostly theistic. Both strategies begin with an engaging experience, usually something from popular media, followed by discussion questions and writing prompts based on the experience. The writing prompts will give you insight into your students' thinking before the unit begins, especially concerns that they have about studying evolution.

If your class is a mix of theistic and nontheistic students, then you probably won't tackle the controversy over evolution right away, which would set a negative tone from the start. The real-life application approach begins

---

theistic evolution, if you're familiar with that approach to resolving the creation/evolution controversy. Theistic evolution is an approach more often associated with deistic, not theistic, religious beliefs.

by answering the question that most students in any class ask: "Why do we have to know this stuff?" To begin this approach, find an experience, in popular media or in current events, for starting the unit that reminds students of how they often encounter evolution in real life. If you choose to start with popular media, have the students actually watch an example of popular media containing references to evolution without much introduction from you. You might simply say, "How often do you hear evolution mentioned in popular media? To get you thinking about that question, I have a movie clip that's an example of what I'm talking about." Then, show them an actual example, such as scenes with references to evolution from movies[3] like *X-Men*, *The Matrix*, or *Planet of the Apes*. You don't need a long clip. Three to five minutes is plenty to get students thinking. After the clip, ask the students to see how many other similar examples they can brainstorm.

If you choose to start the practical applications approach with current events, then ask a question such as "Why do people need to know about evolution to understand some of the current events going on around them? To get you thinking about that question, let me give you an example." Then, present an example, especially one from popular media, showing how knowledge of evolution is required for understanding certain current events. (I wouldn't use the creation/evolution controversy as an example in the real-life application approach, which would stir up controversy right from the start of the unit.) One such example would be a public service announcement[4] communicating to people the need to get the flu vaccine each year because the flu virus is continually evolving. Another example would be a news report, such an archived CNN[5] video, discussing species

---

[3]I found my examples using the Internet Movie Database (www.imdb.com) by searching "evolution" as a keyword and then refining my search to movies. For movies identified, I then went into the Internet Movie Script Database (www.imsdb.com) and searched the scripts for "evolution" to find out how often and where the movie mentioned it.

[4]I found several with the Google keywords "public service announcement flu vaccine."

[5]With the keywords "climate change species," I found "Plight of the Penguins" posted to www.cnn.com/video.

that are threatened by climate change, because species go extinct if they can't evolve quickly enough to adapt to changing climate.

If your students are mostly theistic, then there may be a lot of tension in the room as you begin the study of evolution. Address that tension directly from the start with an approach focused on understanding their concerns. You might start the unit by saying, "I care about you and your worries about studying evolution," a message that you'll repeat throughout the unit. As with the real-life application approach, begin experientially; popular media or current events provide good experiences to start with. With popular media, begin the lesson with a brief statement such as, "I think many of you are concerned about our new unit on evolution. I'm going to show you a movie clip that is a good example to me of the concerns that many people have about evolution. When the clip is over, I'd like to know from you how well you think that clip represents the concerns that people you know have." Then, show a three- to five-minute clip that you have selected because it matches well the concerns that many of your students share. You might find something current from popular media, such as Ben Stein's movie *Expelled*. You should be able to easily find something from current events.[6] If you have access to PBS's video series *Evolution*, I suggest you consider a clip from its seventh video,[7] "What About God?" I found the treatment of the conflict that theistic scientists and students feel to be very respectful and sensitive.

Discussing the Experience

A well-selected experience sets up a discussion with your students. Through the discussion, students begin to get a sense of why they need to study evolution, and you can gain valuable insight into their prior understandings and concerns coming into the unit. You'll use these insights again

---

[6]A quick search on "evolution" in the CNN and Fox archives gave me lots of possibilities.

[7]You can sample scenes from this video at YouTube.com by searching "evolution what about God." Part 4 of video 7 may work well for starting the unit.

and again throughout the unit as you guide your students in constructing a more scientific understanding of evolution.

Tables 3.1 and 3.2 present the flow of two discussion questions you can use to guide the students in examining the engaging experience they just had. Use both focus questions whether you have a few or many resistant students. The order will be different, however. If you have only a few students in your class with objections to evolution, then you'll use discussion question #1 followed by discussion question #2. This order allows you to focus on engaging the most students through the intellectual question "Why do you think evolution is such an important idea in science?" and then assessing students' concerns about studying evolution. In a class where most students have objections, however, start with question #2 so

Table 3.1 The Flow of Discussion Question #1:
"Why do you think evolution is such an important idea in science?"

Segment	Segment Purpose	Starting the Segment	Teacher's Role During the Segment
Announce question	Focus students' attention.	Introduce focus question #1. "Why do you think evolution is such an important idea in science?"	Post the question in a spot visible to all students.
Prime the pump	Help students understand the type of discussion you want to have.	"Think back to what you just experienced. How you would answer the focus question? Feel free to talk about anything you just heard or saw or to bring in your own ideas."	Listen to make sure students answer in depth and with their own ideas, not ideas that they think they're supposed to say. Redirect if students appear to be answering a different question than the one posed, including raising objections about evolution.
Pair and share	Help each student get ideas flowing.	"Pair up with someone and talk through your own answer to the focus question."	Move through the room and make sure students are on task. Listen to get a beginning idea of what all students are thinking.
Individual responses	Help students clarify their own thinking.	"Write out your own response to the focus question. Take some time with this and write your thoughts in detail."	Move through the room and make sure students are on task. Over their shoulders, quickly scan selected students' responses to get an idea of their understanding.
Large-group discussion	Determine students' ideational allegiances.	"I'd like to hear what one of you wrote. While that person reads, I want everyone else to listen carefully." After one student responds, "Raise your hand if you wrote something similar to what we just heard." "Now, who has a different idea they would like to read?" After a student responds, "Raise your hand if you wrote something similar." Repeat until almost all students have shown an allegiance to an announced idea.	Monitor student behavior to make sure all students are listening respectfully. Make notes about the students' main ideas and a rough number of how many students believe each main idea. Show no value on any particular idea and give no indication of whether ideas are correct or incorrect.

**Table 3.2   The Flow of Discussion Question #2:
"What concerns you about studying evolution?"**

Segment	Segment Purpose	Starting the Segment	Teacher's Role During the Segment
Prime the pump	Help students understand the type of discussion you want to have.	"Evolution can be an uncomfortable topic for many people. I'd like to hear the concerns people raise about studying evolution. I'm not asking you to talk about your own beliefs, unless you really want to. Instead, I'd like to hear from you the concerns of people you know."	Model respect and tolerance for people who object to evolution. Help students see that you really do want them to be honest with you about potential concerns. Redirect if students appear to be answering a different question than the one posed, including raising objections about evolution.
Pair and share	Help each student get ideas flowing.	"Pair up with someone and brainstorm a list of the concerns that people have about studying evolution. Each of you should write your own copy of your list."	Move through the room and make sure students are on task. Watch carefully for students who are reluctant to engage in the discussion.
Announce question	Focus students' work.	Introduce focus question #2. "What concerns you about studying evolution?"	Post the question in a spot visible to all students.
Individual responses	Help students clarify their own thinking.	"Now, I want to know what concerns you have individually, and I'm going to give you a chance to respond to me anonymously. Take two index cards and spread out through the room so that each of you can write privately. Write on the first index card the biggest concern you have as we start studying evolution. If you have a second big concern, write it on the other card. I'm the only one who will ever read this card. If you don't have any concerns about studying evolution, then please tell me that on your card and write a note about what you hope to get out of studying evolution."	Move through the room and make sure students are on task. Protect students' privacy. Collect cards directly from the students when they're done to protect their anonymity.
Analysis	Determine students' ideational allegiances.	[N/A: This analysis is done outside of class.]	Sort the students' responses into stacks of those that are similar. Make notes on their concerns for use later in the unit.

that they know from the beginning that you are sensitive to their concerns. Then follow up with another discussion around question #1, so that you can begin the process of guiding students to think about the scientific value of evolution.

The discussion in Table 3.1 begins by announcing and posting the focus question and then letting a few students give their initial responses. I call that segment "priming the pump." Old hand pumps from years ago wouldn't start pumping water unless they were primed with a little bit of water. In the same way, often the ideas in a classroom discussion don't start flowing well until two or three ideas get thrown out in front of the class. As shown in detail in Table 3.1, after you prime the pump and get the ideas flowing, the students then move through a sequence of small-group and individual activities to fully engage them. Students first work in pairs so that everyone gets a chance to talk, and then they write their own responses individually to get their own thinking out in such a way as to clarify their ideas. While they are talking and writing, move around among them to make sure that they're on task and to get a sense of what their ideas are. I usually keep a clipboard, paper, and a pen with me so that I can make notes on what I hear.

The last segment of discussion question #1 has you facilitate a large-group discussion in which several students report their individual ideas while you try to get a rough sense of the number of students aligned with each idea. It's important during this discussion to maintain your best poker face and not let students know that you think any idea expressed is more correct than others. If you do let on that you think their ideas are wrong, students will go from expressing what they think to watching your cues and trying to give the answer you're looking for. They'll find out later in the unit what the scientific ideas are; right now, you want to know what their ideas are. Keep in mind also that you're trying to get a sense of the ideas that most students, but not all, have allegiance to. You don't have to listen to every single idea. That would take too much time, and it's not the point of the segment. Instead, simply say to yourself something like, "OK. I'm hearing three different ideas. About two-thirds of the students believe idea A, and the rest are split between ideas B and C." Make sure you have good notes that you can go back to during the rest of the unit. In the past, I've used a blank overhead transparency where I write the students' main ideas. Now, with newer technology, I tend to post the students' thinking to my whiteboard, take a digital picture or video of it with my cell phone, and save the picture on my Mac so I can refer back to it later.

Discussion question #2 has a similar flow, but you'll see some differences in Table 3.2 that are designed to protect students from feeling like they have to talk aloud about uncomfortable ideas. The discussion begins with a question designed so that students don't have to talk about their own personal ideas. Instead, you direct them to describe the concerns of someone they know. Make sure as you prime the pump on this discussion that your words and body language make clear to them that you respect their personal beliefs and that you really want to know their thoughts and feeling. As with discussion question #1, use your best poker face and don't tip them off to the value you place on anything they say. During the pair-and-share segment in Table 3.2, again, the students aren't asked to talk about and list their personal concerns, but instead concerns that people in general have about evolution. Finally, at that point you're ready to announce and post the actual focus question. By waiting, you've given the students a chance to warm up to the discussion before getting them to focus on their own concerns. Once you've given them the directions for the next segment and they've spread out in the room to begin writing, it's essential that you enforce strict privacy about ideas. You should go to the students individually and collect the cards so that students aren't up and moving past anyone still writing.

The analysis segment of Table 3.2 is done outside of class. Read each card and make stacks of cards expressing similar ideas. You don't need to be rigorous in deciding how to stack the cards. Precision in sorting is not the point. Instead, the point is to understand the main concerns your students have and a rough percentage of how many students feel that concern. As with discussion question #1, you're looking for a general summary such as, "My students have about five different personal concerns about studying evolution. About half of the students expressed concern A, about a fourth expressed concerns B and C, and just a few expressed concerns C and D. About a third of my students said they weren't concerned about studying evolution." Before you start sorting, though, decide whether you're going to keep the cards from your different classes separate or pool them all together. If you pool them, you'll have an overall sense of your students' concerns across all of the periods you teach, but you won't know if differences exist between your classes. If you don't pool them, you have to keep track of a different summary for each class. I usually pool my students' ideas across all my classes, but before doing so, I make a mark on each card to indicate which class it came from in case later I want to separate them out by period.

Introducing the Unit Essential Question

You've given students an engaging experience, and you've guided them through two rounds of discussions as they reacted both to that experience and to their prior experiences with evolution itself. You haven't introduced any of the scientific content yet, but all students should be pondering why understanding evolution is important. Students with conflicts should sense that you will provide a safe environment for them. They may not, however, be fully engaged in the scientific nature of the question, especially if some of them think that you might be setting up a debate of sorts about whether evolution is scientifically correct or not. The last part of engagement, then, is to solidify their focus on the actual science involved. For that, deploy the essential question discussed in the previous chapter: "Why can't we just skip evolution?" Your students are ready now to examine this question for the first time. You'll return to the essential question several times throughout the unit, so there's no need for a lengthy discussion now. Instead, get students to begin considering the question. Table 3.3 shows the flow of the discussion of the essential question. You'll see many features similar to those of the two earlier discussions, but here I suggest a small-group discussion, rather than in pairs, to add some variety to the discussion format.

In the large-group discussion, for the first time in the unit, you'll bring your knowledge of science into the discussion. The point of the discussion should still be students sharing their ideas, but at times you'll ask a question or bring up a thought to help them think more deeply about the importance of studying evolution. Use your position as a teacher to continue to affirm resistant students in the concerns that they have about studying evolution, but gently draw out those concerns into the classroom. The final segment has students writing their initial individual reflections on the essential question. Later in the unit, you can direct students back to these thoughts with metacognition to see how their ideas have changed.

Table 3.3 The Flow of the Essential Question Discussion:
"Why can't we just skip evolution?"

Segment	Segment Purpose	Starting the Segment	Teacher's Role During the Segment
Announce question	Focus students' attention.	Introduce the essential question.	Post the question in a spot visible to all students.
Prime the pump	Help students understand the type of discussion you want to have.	"Take a look at the essential question for our unit on evolution. I've heard many students ask a question similar to this when they face evolution. Based on the discussion we had yesterday, how would you answer the essential question? Can a few of you get us started with your first reaction to the question?"	Listen to make sure students are answering in depth, connecting their own ideas with their tentative understandings of why evolution is important in science. Redirect if students appear to be answering a different question than the one posed.
Small-group discussion	Help each student get ideas flowing.	"In groups of three or four, talk about how you would answer the essential question right now. Be ready to report your discussion to the whole class. Some of you have concerns about studying evolution. Feel free to work those into your answer to the essential question."	Move through the room and make sure students are on task. Listen to get an idea of how students answer the question. Redirect any groups that get sidetracked into a discussion of objections to evolution.
Large-group discussion	Guide students collectively to begin to see the importance of studying evolution.	"Raise your hand and, when I call on you, tell me just one idea that hasn't yet been mentioned. I'll list it on the board, and I want you to keep the same list in your notes."	Facilitate the discussion well. Occasionally offer expert insight to help students sharpen their initial understanding so that they see how the study of evolution is important and valuable. Listen for and make notes of misconceptions they may hold about evolution.
Individual reflection	Guide students individually to begin to see the importance of studying evolution.	"Think how you would personally and individually answer the question. Think about everything you've seen and heard about evolution thus far. Spend about five minutes writing in your notebook about your current thinking and how you would answer the essential question individually. Remember, I'm not looking for any kind of right answer from you now; instead, write about what you think."	Move through the room and make sure students are on task. Over their shoulders, review selected students' responses to get an idea of their individual engagement.

Dealing with Objections

Objections are a tough issue when your goal is to teach evolution in such a way that your resistant theistic students feel as little threat as possible. If these students sense from you that you're not willing to listen to their objections, then they may hear the message, "Check your faith at the door. This is a science class. We don't talk about that kind of stuff in here." On the other hand, if you give too much credence to objections, then you risk allowing student concerns to derail the teaching of essential science content.

Following is a list of typical objections to evolution, based on my experience listening to people raise objections about evolution and on research I did on a few sites focused on the creation/evolution controversy. The chief sites I drew from were the "Resources" section of the website of the Institute for Creation Research (www.icr.org/ICR-Resources), the "Get Answers" section at AnswersInGenesis.Org, and "An Index to Creationist Claims" at TalkOrigins.Org. You may want to make note of the objections that you typically hear from your students or ones that I didn't include that you expect your students to raise.

Typical Objections to Evolution

- The Earth is a lot younger than scientists say. All of that carbon dating stuff can't be trusted because it gives the wrong dates.
- There are just too many missing links for evolution to be true.
- Evolution is just a theory.
- Everything evolutionists think happened is really a result of Noah's flood.
- The Earth is only six thousand years old, and that's not enough time for everything to have evolved.
- There's just no way that life evolved. You can't get living stuff from nonliving stuff.
- If everything evolved because of survival of the fittest, then why do we have anything good around us? Why is the world so awesomely beautiful?
- Isn't science a search for truth?
- Fossils have been found that prove that people and dinosaurs lived at the same time.
- Didn't scientists make up some fossils that are supposed to prove people evolved?
- You just can't get complex life from simple life forms.
- There's no way that something as complex as the eye could have just evolved. It has too many parts.
- Aren't peppered moths fake?

- No one has ever seen macroevolution really happen.
- Don't scientists themselves disagree about whether evolution really happened?
- If evolution is true, then we'd have a whole lot more fossils out there to show how one species became another.
- The moon has just a little bit of dust, so the Earth can't be six billion years old.
- The second law of thermodynamics says that evolution couldn't happen.

Dealing with objections productively is difficult until your resistant students have a clear sense of how you want them to understand the scientific evidence for evolution, but not necessarily accept it. That sense may not come until later in the unit, however, and I won't address objections directly until Chapter 6. Until that point in the unit, I suggest that you listen to students' objections, briefly acknowledge them by posting them to a public list you'll keep in your room, and then move forward with teaching the lesson. In doing so, you'll bit by bit build a list of objections and you'll allow students to state concerns that are important to them, but you'll keep the focus on building the necessary foundations for effectively examining those objections through many lessons about the evidence for evolution. Deferring discussion of objections will be difficult for some students at times. Middle schoolers in general struggle with impatience; they will have a hard time waiting. Resistant students who accept creationist claims may feel compelled to raise objections. Nevertheless, gently but firmly require that students wait, consistently affirming that you will eventually address their objections, but not until you know that the time is right.

In these engagement lessons, students may or may not raise objections. If they do, simply say to them something like, "That's an objection to evolution. I hear you, but I'd like you to hold off on discussing that today." Doing so keeps the focus of these lessons on engaging students versus the disengagement that often occurs from the creation/evolution controversy. Also, such simple, clear instruction allows you to set the tone that you will determine the time when the class discusses objections.

Summary

With the discussions described in this chapter completed, you've begun the process of teaching evolution using both inquiry and an approach that engages resistant students without threatening their beliefs. Your students should show some curiosity about the upcoming lessons about evolution. Some may want to know more about the science itself. Others may be more interested in how you're going to teach the unit, realizing that although you're not stifling the concerns that resistant students have, you're also not teaching creationism. They don't yet have a clear answer to the unit's essential question, but each of your students has begun the process of thinking about why she or he needs to study evolution instead of just skipping it. They're ready for their first formal lessons in the actual scientific evidence for evolution.

4

Guiding Students to Examine the Evidence for Evolution

You're now ready to begin the formal study of evolution, and you'll guide your theistic students in a study that many may feel challenges some of their core beliefs. Some students are probably holding their breath, wondering what's going to happen next, and you may be doing the same thing! Critical issues are how best to begin the study of evolution so that all of your students learn well and so that your resistant students can enter the study as successfully as possible. Inquiry offers effective guidance on both of those issues because it begins with examination of scientific evidence. Inquiry guides all students to build their understanding of the powerful ideas of science, such as evolution, based on the facts supporting those ideas. For your resistant students, looking first at the evidence avoids pitting evolution against their beliefs in a battle over which is true.

A key difference between inquiry and traditional science teaching is the use of evidence. A biology teacher could lecture on the structure and function of cellular organelles without ever giving students any evidence for how cell biologists know what's in a cell and how they know the function each organelle plays. A physics teacher could teach Newton's laws of motion without ever providing students with any evidence for the laws and how we know that they describe well motion in the world around us. Traditional science teaching focuses students on the explanations of science, but often divorces those explanations from the evidence from which they developed.

Inquiry places evidence at the center of the science classroom. In inquiry-based lessons, teachers guide students to examine evidence that they or others have collected. This is essential feature #2 of inquiry:

> *Learners give priority to evidence, which allows them to develop and evaluate explanations that address scientifically oriented questions.* . . . Science distinguishes itself from other ways of knowing through use of empirical evidence as the basis for explanations about how the natural world works. Scientists concentrate on getting accurate data from observations of phenomena. . . . In some instances, scientists can control conditions to obtain their evidence; in other instances they cannot control the conditions or control would distort the phenomena. . . .
>
> In their classroom inquiries, students use evidence to develop explanations for scientific phenomena. They observe plants, animal, and rocks, and carefully describe their characteristics. They take measurements of temperature, distances, and time, and carefully record them. . . . Or they obtain evidence from their teacher, instructional materials, the Web, or elsewhere, to "fuel" their inquiries. (National Research Council 2000, 25–26)

Inquiry places high value on students' collecting evidence themselves so that they learn the associated processes of science, such as carefully following procedures and recording data accurately. Through the process of collecting data, students learn that their data are trustworthy, and they build confidence that scientific evidence in general is believable. Inquiry doesn't require, however, that students collect all of the data that they examine. As you can imagine, this is good news for you and the evidence for evolution you want your students to examine. You really can't redo every fossil dig ever conducted by paleontologists! Students can, however, examine the evidence already collected about evolution.

In teaching evolution, giving priority to evidence, as required by inquiry, is a key approach for lessening the controversy in your classroom. You don't stand at the center of your class and say, "Believe evolution because I say so!" or because scientists say so, or because of any other appeal to authority. Instead, you put the evidence in front of the students and guide them to see how evolution has developed as the best scientific explanation for the evidence.

This chapter will guide you in selecting the evidence that you'll put in front of your students. Two sample lessons are included that will help you introduce evolution to your students using an inquiry-based approach. One lesson focuses on the evidence for natural selection; the other, on the evidence for evolution itself. We also look at how to accommodate resistant students during these lessons so that you minimize the chance that they get turned off from learning at the very start of the unit. I briefly mention how to guide students to begin to explain the evidence they encounter, but the bulk of that process is addressed in the next two chapters.

Selecting the Evidence for Students to Examine

It may feel like swimming against the current when you try to find evidence for natural selection and evolution. Many of the resources that I've examined focus on the ideas of evolution without supporting those explanations richly with evidence from the natural world. No wonder so many people are skeptical about evolution! They're being asked to accept a scientific idea without its proof.

Begin with your students' textbook. Examine the chapters on evolution for presentation of actual scientific evidence. Sadly, if your textbook is typical of those in U.S. schools, you won't find much evidence at all, if any. If you have any other textbooks on hand, examine them also. College biology textbooks are a source to consider, especially if you still have them from your college training.

Web-based resources are another good choice. Keep in mind that you're looking for actual evidence of evolution and natural selection. It is easy to get lost when you start an extensive Web search. This happened to me as I looked for evidence for natural selection and evolution. I drifted away from my goal of finding scientific data. Bookmarking good sites into a folder can help keep you focused and keep you from wasting a lot of time wandering off target.

As an example of evidence for natural selection, see John W. Kimball's Biology Page on Speciation[1] (Google keywords: Darwin's finches specia-

---

[1] http://users.rcn.com/jkimball.ma.ultranet/BiologyPages/S/Speciation.html.

tion). The page employs Darwin's finches as an example of how several species can develop from one, and the page uses evidence to support that explanation. The evidence on the page isn't extensive, but it does describe how beak structure, diet, and behavior of the Galapagos finches provide evidence for how the different species developed by the process of natural selection.

The sample lesson on natural selection later in this chapter uses a jigsaw approach in guiding students to examine the evidence for natural selection from four species. I recommend that you set four different organisms as your target for your search. Keep in mind that this is an introductory lesson, so you're not looking for extensive evidence. The students will move through each of the four species fairly quickly, and they'll compile the evidence from the species into one graphic organizer. Look for resources, such as a Web page or a handout made from a photocopy out of a book, that give students a snapshot of the evidence for how natural selection has been at play in the development of four different organisms. In a class of twenty-four students, you would need two or three copies of the resources for each of the four organisms, for a total of eight to twelve resource sets.[2]

The second sample lesson is not a jigsaw lesson, however. It is on evolution, and for it you need only one example of clear evidence of how a species has evolved from another species. Select an example where the evidence is strong that the process resulted in a descendent quite different than the ancestor (unlike Darwin's finches where natural selection produced different kinds of the same species). Whale evolution is a good example for this kind of descent over time. Again, examine your students' textbook or any other texts you have on hand for evidence that you can place in front of your students, but don't be surprised if you find that the evidence for evolution in textbooks is weak or nonexistent.

I found several online resources that presented well the evidence for whale evolution. The best one for use in the introductory lesson described

----

[2]With a class of twenty-four students, I have them work in six groups of four students each. To jigsaw them, they would break out into four groups of six students each.

later is Edward T. Babinski's The Evolution of Whales,[3] which is an adaptation of a 2001 article from *National Geographic* (Google keywords: Babinski "the whale tale"). The page is extensive, and it consistently employs evidence to argue for the development of modern whales from *Pakicetus,* a four-legged, terrestrial mammal that lived fifty million years ago. Your school's media center might have the actual issue of *National Geographic* that Mr. Babinski based his Web page on. If so, you can use the original article rather than the Web page in developing a resource for your students to use.

The Appendix may also give you some additional help in finding good resources that you can tap. The evidence for natural selection and evolution is abundant and clear, but you'll have to hunt to find it since most American educational resources focus on explanation without evidence. With evidence, however, you'll lessen some of the controversy in your classroom because you'll ask students to make sense of actual scientific evidence rather than simply take your word that evolution occurred.

Guiding Students to Examine the Evidence for Natural Selection

Table 4.1 presents the outline of an inquiry-based lesson you can use for introducing your students to the evidence for natural selection. This lesson is conceptualized as a jigsaw lesson in which the students break out from their regular groups to examine the evidence for natural selection in the four organisms you have identified, as described earlier. (If you're not familiar with the jigsaw approach to cooperative learning, several excellent descriptions are available online. I suggest Elliot Aronson's Jigsaw Classroom at www.jigsaw.org.) Then students return to their regular groups, with each student acting as an expert on the species he or she learned about in the jigsaw group.

Take a look at the lesson outline in Table 4.1. The lesson is broken down into segments corresponding to the five essential features of inquiry. The

[3]http://www.edwardtbabinski.us/whales/evolution_of_whales/.

lesson begins with engaging the students (essential feature #1) by asking them about their understanding of the evidence for natural selection. The students then give priority to evidence (essential feature #2) in jigsaw cooperative learning, using the resources you've prepared. The students next develop explanations for the evidence they encountered (essential feature #3) by reflecting individually and in their small groups on their original understandings of the evidence for evolution in light of the new evidence they encountered in this lesson. They continue this reflection in large-group discussion so that they can evaluate their explanations in light of alternative explanations (essential feature #4). They end the lesson by communicating and justifying their explanations (essential feature #5) via metacognition as they individually write about how their ideas have changed about the evidence for natural selection. All of the subsequent lesson outlines follow the same structure so that you can clearly see how to implement inquiry during the unit.

The first part of the lesson focuses on activating and assessing student prior knowledge. Reexamining Table 2.3, the benchmarks for natural selection, may help you to see the big ideas that your students should be coming in with from their prior studies. Middle school students should begin the lesson with an understanding that individuals of a species are different and that those differences give some individuals advantages for survival in particular environments or during environmental changes. High school students should enter the lesson with a deeper understanding of these ideas, especially how specific traits give individuals advantages, how competition affects survival, and how environmental changes can impact whole species. Your students may or may not have these understandings, and one of the purposes of the first lesson segment is to allow you to assess how much prior knowledge your students actually have.

In the third, fourth, and fifth segments of the lesson, students discuss evidence with their peers and examine their own understanding in light of the evidence presented. These discussions are central to an inquiry-based approach because learners formulate explanations from evidence. As you look through the lesson segments, note that your role is to guide them in productive small- and large-group discussion of the evidence they've encountered. Guiding these types of discussion is central to the pedagogy

Table 4.1 Lesson Outline of the Evidence for Natural Selection

Examining the Focus Question: "What Is the Evidence for Natural Selection?"

(Learners Engage in a Scientific Question)

Lesson Segments	Accommodations for Resistant Students
■ Ask students, "What is natural selection?" Engage the students in a brief, large-group conversation in which you activate their prior knowledge about natural selection.	■ If students object to the validity of natural selection, especially due to their other beliefs, post their concerns to the parking lot. Make sure students know that you're listening well to them and not ignoring their concerns, but you are holding off for now on addressing those concerns. You may want to say simply, "I hear the objection you're raising, and I'm posting it to the parking lot for now."
■ Introduce the focus question for this lesson, directing students to where you've posted it. Ask students to individually brainstorm a list in their notebooks of the evidence they know for natural selection.	
■ Direct students to continue brainstorming in their small groups and to expand their list based on new instances of evidence mentioned by other group members.	
■ Guide a large-group discussion during which you create a whole-class summary list of students' ideas about the evidence for natural selection.	
■ Ask students, "What questions do you have about the evidence for natural selection?" Make note of their responses and any misconceptions revealed thus far throughout the lesson.	
■ Assess student prior knowledge about natural selection revealed thus far and the questions they raised about natural selection. Decide how you will adjust the pace of the lesson to best meet their needs.	

Examination of the Evidence

(Learners Give Priority to Evidence)

■ Describe briefly the instructions for the jigsaw stage of the lesson, making sure the students see the connection between the work they will do and the focus question. Direct students as they prepare themselves as experts on the species that their jigsaw group is examining.	■ Monitor the engagement of students you think may have objections to studying evolution. Don't push them to engage. Instead, determine their comfort level with examining the scientific evidence. Are they removing themselves from the assigned work? Are they peripherally involved? Are they completing the work, but remaining quiet in the group?
■ As each jigsaw group examines the evidence for natural selection for their assigned species, walk around and monitor the interactions to make sure students are on task and productive.	
■ After ten to fifteen minutes in jigsaw groups, have students return to their regular groups. Instruct the students in the type of discussion you want them to have so that each group member reports on the species they studied in jigsaw.	
■ As the groups work, walk around and monitor their interactions to make sure students are on task and productive.	

used in this book. Note the types of process skills that your students must have to learn via inquiry, such as abilities for collaborating with their peers, following instructions, and engaging in respectful dialogue. They'll also need abilities for basing scientific conclusions on data and following the logic of scientific arguments. Whether your students already have these skills or not will influence the pace at which you'll be able to proceed with lessons in the unit.

Table 4.1 *Continued*

Small-Group Discussion of Evidence Encountered
(Learners Develop Explanations Based on Evidence)

Lesson Segments

- Ask the students to review the list they created at the beginning of the lesson in answer to the focus question. Ask them to ponder silently the question "How has my thinking changed since I created that list?"
- Prime the pump by asking for two or three students' responses.
- Direct students to discuss in small groups their individual answers regarding how their thinking has changed.
- After students examine their original understanding, ask all of them to write in their science notebooks two or three sentences about how their thinking changed.

Accommodations for Resistant Students

- Continue to monitor the engagement of your resistant students as you move among groups. How willing are they to participate in their group's discussion? Are they being combative or passive-aggressive? Are they perhaps asking questions but not volunteering their own understanding?
- As the students write about how their ideas have changed, walk around and review responses, being careful not to single out your resistant students' responses for review. Instead, attend to their responses as part of attending to all students' responses.

Large-Group Discussion of Evidence Encountered
(Learners Evaluate Their Explanations)

- Ask several students to read or paraphrase for the whole class what they wrote about how their thinking has changed. Listen to several student responses.
- Make a statement such as "Now, I'm curious about questions that have come to your mind about the evidence for natural selection."
- Guide a large-group discussion in which students brainstorm questions that come to mind. Post as many questions as you can to a public list.

- If students raise objections, invite them to convert their objections into questions, then post their questions along with the other questions students are raising. If they're not willing to convert their objections, then post them to the parking lot. Let students know that you accept and honor their unwillingness to convert their objections.

Lesson Reflections
(Learners Communicate and Justify Their Explanations)

- Briefly describe for students the important distinction between scientific evidence and explanation. Point out and label questions on the public list that focus on evidence and those that focus on explanations.
- Describe for the students how you began the unit, not with evolutionary theory (i.e. an explanation), but with evidence, beginning in the place science must always start.
- Ask students to consider the question "How helpful was it for you that we began our study of natural selection with actual scientific evidence?" Direct students to write two or three sentences in answer to that question in their science notebooks. As they write, move around the room, noting any themes in their responses.

- Determine in advance of teaching the lesson how much you will say now about the objections in the parking lot. You'll come back to these objections in later lessons, but you'll determine now how much to say about that plan based on your students' tolerance for waiting and the intensity of their objections. Make sure they know that they can trust you when you say that you will truly come back to these important ideas.

Accommodating Resistant Students During Inquiry

Table 4.1 also shows how to accommodate the needs of resistant students during each segment of the lesson. This first lesson begins to establish an intellectually safe environment. Some students may want to participate very little, and you're going to allow that for now. Others will want to raise objections, questions, and concerns, and by the end of the lesson, they should know that you're listening to them. I do not recommend any kind of intervention at this early point in the unit for students refusing to participate at all. Instead, I recommend that you allow resistant students to engage to the level that they are comfortable with, even if that's silence or refusal to complete the task. Your goal is to invite them into the unit's study by signaling to them how strongly you are committed to creating an intellectually safe environment for them. If they continue to refuse to participate in later lessons, you will need to intervene, but that can wait for now.

Also note how the lesson structure provides you many opportunities to gauge the level of resistance that students display. Most resistant students will probably not be overt, and you should simply watch them and learn the level of involvement that they're comfortable with at this point. Make notes of any concerns they express during group work. Use what you learn here in revising later lessons in the unit in hopes to continue inviting them into the study of evolution.

The parking lot used in Table 4.1 is simply an area for posting ideas to hold, or park, for now and return to later. You may have participated in a professional development session where the facilitator used a parking lot. For your class, the parking lot could be an area of your whiteboard, but that ties up board space. Instead, I use a piece of flip-chart paper or butcher paper tacked to a space of blank wall so that the ideas are posted and available throughout the unit and my board is free for other tasks. In setting up your parking lot, think through how you want to handle objections raised by different classes. For example, do you want fifth-period students to see the objections raised by second-period students? That becomes confusing on several different fronts.

The first time you use the parking lot, explain to the students what you are doing, especially how you are saving their objections, not dismissing them. Another reason for parking objections at this point is that most are explanations (e.g., "Well, my preacher says that God made the animals by kinds, and kinds don't change."), and the class is not in explanation mode yet. Explanations are the focus of the next lessons, but for now, have students focus first on the evidence. Scientific explanations must develop from scientific evidence, and you can emphasize that point by redirecting away from explanations until your students have begun with the foundation of actual evidence.

Guiding Students to Examine the Evidence for Evolution

The next lesson continues the plan of starting with evidence, not explanations, and beginning with a big picture, not details. It focuses blatantly on evolution, though, which is a land mine for many resistant students, whereas natural selection often isn't. Because of the high potential for conflict as you introduce evidence for evolution, the structure for this second lesson is similar to the first lesson. Many resistant students struggle with the content of the lesson; they don't need to struggle with the process of the lesson itself as well.

The lesson outline in Table 4.2 follows the same inquiry structure as the lesson on natural selection. Students engage in a focus question (essential feature #1), they examine evidence that you provide (essential feature #2), they discuss in small and large groups how that evidence challenges their initial understanding (essential features #3 and #4), and they communicate and justify their explanations via metacognition on their initial understanding (essential feature #5).

Unlike the first lesson, this lesson does not employ a jigsaw. Instead, it focuses on all students examining the same evidence for evolution. As mentioned previously, you could focus the lesson on whale evolution because of the strength of the evidence in the series between *Pakicetus* and modern whales. You may decide to present evidence of evolution from a different species. The lesson outline works with whatever species you choose, as long as you focus students on the evidence itself. As a reminder, create a resource sheet for students to use during the lesson that gives them the key evidence describing the evolution of the species you select.

Give students instructions that clearly point them to examining the evidence and holding off on evolutionary explanations for now. You could do this by having each student group construct a graphic organizer showing the key evidence involved in the evolutionary series the group is examining.

Table 4.2 Lesson Outline of the Evidence for Evolution

Examining the Focus Question: "What Is the Evidence for Evolution?"
(Learners Engage in a Scientific Question)

Lesson Segments

- Ask several students to read or paraphrase their final reflections from the previous lesson. Review that lesson briefly, if needed.
- Introduce the focus question for this lesson, directing students to where you've posted it. Ask students a question such as, "Is this question a harder one to examine than the one for natural selection?" Hear several of their responses.
- Ask students individually to brainstorm a list in their science notebooks of the evidence they know for evolution. Monitor their work to see how difficult this task is for them and to make sure that they are listing actual scientific evidence.
- Have students continue brainstorming in small groups and expand their list based on new instances of evidence mentioned by other group members.
- Guide a large-group discussion during which you create a whole-class summary list of student ideas about the evidence for evolution. Remind students of the previous distinction between evidence and explanation and how, for now, the focus is on actual scientific evidence for evolution.
- Ask students, "Was this list harder to generate than the list for natural selection? Why or why not?" Listen to several of their responses, making notes of any misconceptions revealed thus far throughout the lesson.
- Assess the amount of student prior knowledge about evolution revealed and decide how you will adjust the pace of the lesson.

Accommodations for Resistant Students

- Continue the same procedure from the previous lesson of posting objections to the parking lot. Don't make any distinctions, however, between religious objections and objections of any other type.

Examination of the Evidence
(Learners Give Priority to Evidence)

- Introduce the inquiry briefly, making sure the students see the connection between the work they will do and the focus question.
- Instruct the students in the type of discussion you want them to have about the evidence for evolution that you're asking them to review, including the use of a graphic organizer if you opt for that.
- As the groups work, walk around and monitor their interactions to make sure that they're on task and productive.

- Continue to monitor the engagement of students you think may have objections, but don't intervene. Are they removing themselves from the task now that the focus is blatantly on evolution? Are they completing the assignment, but maintaining an intellectual distance from the content?

Figure 4.1 gives a mock-up of such a graphic organizer. For each species in the series that students review, they will list its name, draw or record what they consider to be the most important pieces of evidence scientist have for the existence of that species, and record the date that evidence is found in the fossil record. The use of a graphic organizer requiring the students to distill out the evidence keeps the students focused on the evidence, and the completed organizer becomes a foundation for future lessons when you want to remind students that all scientific explanations must be grounded in scientific data. If you teach middle school students or students unfamiliar with learning by inquiry, you might scaffold the graphic organizer by

Table 4.2   *Continued*

Small-Group Discussion of Evidence Encountered
(Learners Develop Explanations Based on Evidence)

Lesson Segments

- Ask the students to review the list they created at the beginning of the lesson in answer to the focus question. Ask them to ponder silently the question "How has my thinking changed?"
- Direct students to discuss in small groups their individual answers to the questions.
- After they examine their original understanding, ask students to write in their science notebooks two or three sentences about how their thinking has changed.

Accommodations for Resistant Students

- Continue monitoring the engagement of your resistant students.
- If your resistant students disengage, note the reactions of their classmates, especially the students in their small group.
- As you review the students' written responses, ponder how you will respectfully respond to objections they might raise.

Large-Group Discussion of Evidence Encountered
(Learners Evaluate Their Explanations)

- Listen to several students read or paraphrase for the whole class what they wrote about how their thinking has changed.
- Make a statement such as, "Now, I'm curious about questions that have come to your mind about the evidence for evolution."
- Guide a large-group discussion in which students brainstorm questions that come to mind. Post as many questions as you can to a public list.

- Continue the procedure from the previous lesson of inviting students to convert objections into questions, but accepting objections that they don't want to convert. Post objections to the parking lot.

Lesson Reflections
(Learners Communicate and Justify Their Explanations)

- If necessary, review the distinction between scientific evidence and explanation. Point out and label items from the public list of questions that focus on evidence and those that focus on explanations. Remind the students how you began the unit with evidence, not explanations.
- Ask students to consider the question "How helpful was it for you that we began our study of evolution with actual scientific evidence?" Have students write two or three sentences in answer to that question in their science notebooks. As they write, move around the room, noting any themes in their responses.
- Ask any students who are willing to read or paraphrase their responses.

- Implement your plan for how much you will say now about the objections in the parking lot, continuing your focus on building the trust of resistant students by truly honoring their concerns.

---

replacing "Species 1" with the actual species name that you want to focus on and by limiting the number of species to only three or four that you think are the most important. This type of scaffolding keeps students from being overwhelmed by the amount of information in the resource.

As with the lesson on natural selection, this lesson provides you many opportunities to listen to your students' prior ideas about evolution. Review Table 2.2, the benchmarks for biological evolution, to get a sense of the ideas your students should have when they first enter the lesson. Middle schoolers should be aware of fossil evidence and how it contributes to our understanding of the similarities and differences between today's life-forms and

	Species Name	Key Evidence	Date of Evidence
Species 1			
Species 2			
Species 3			
. . .			

Figure 4.1 Graphic Organizer for Evolution Evidence

those of the past. High schoolers should have a more refined understanding of the contributions of fossils, including how they form and how fossil evidence helps scientists understand the history of Earth's life-forms. As the lesson progresses, listen to your students to see how much of this prior knowledge they truly have and to hear what misconceptions about evolution they reveal by what they say or the questions they ask. Adjust future lessons to fill in holes in their prior knowledge or to address specific misconceptions that your students have.

Note also that the lesson focuses on the students' simply encountering evidence for evolution, not solidifying their understanding of how all of the pieces of evidence fit together. Later lessons provide more opportunities for students to return to the kind of evidence presented in this lesson to get a better sense of how all of the pieces do fit. I even suggest that students come back specifically to the resource and graphic organizer for this lesson and go deeper. For now, though, the students need mainly to become used to having discussions about evolution based on evidence, not opinion. Guide them in how to discuss evolution from a scientific basis, and lay the foundation for future lessons in which you help students step back from the specifics about evolution and natural selection and look at the bigger picture of the scientific worldview.

For your resistant students, continue to establish an intellectually safe environment where they know that you're willing to hear their questions, concerns, and objections. Continue to use the parking lot for objections, but also continue to assure your students that you really are coming back to these objections later when the focus shifts to scientific explanations. Continue to monitor the engagement of your students to gain a sense of which are struggling with the topic due to their other beliefs, but do so without calling any special attention to them.

Continue also allowing resistant students to engage at whatever level makes them comfortable and expecting them to proceed through the lesson cautiously. As you're probably well aware, when teachers say the "E word," many resistant students significantly raise their guard. Inquiry may actually create a higher level of conflict because you're asking them to engage in individual and small-group work directly related to evolution. You're not simply lecturing and allowing them to ignore you if they want. The lesson will be successful if your students simply dip their toes in the water of evolution and realize that you're not going to let them get pulled under by a big wave.

Summary

Through these lessons, your students encounter natural selection and evolution in the context of an evidence-based lesson. Rather than learning evolution as an idea important just because scientists say so, they begin where all science must start—with actual scientific data. You also carefully control the environment for your resistant students. You set the tone that you're not going to allow objections raised by vocal students derail your responsibility to teach evolution. At the same time, you show by your actions that you notice and care if they're worried, threatened, or disengaged.

The next chapter addresses how to create lessons that help students understand the theory of evolution itself as you move forward to essential feature #3. Consider what other lessons you need to create before moving forward. Reexamine Tables 2.2 and 2.3 to see if your students have significant gaps in their prior knowledge. If so, create lessons specifically focused on closing those gaps so that future lessons won't bog down. Do your students struggle with the process of inquiry itself, either the examination of evidence or the small- and large-group discussions inherent in inquiry? If so, create a few lessons that give them additional experience with those processes so that they are more skilled before they encounter the sometimes tough process work ahead. Also, consider now the requirements of your state, district, and local curricula. If you have required content that doesn't appear in Tables 2.4 and 2.5, the Final Unit Focus tables, you'll need to consider where to insert that content. Now would be a good time to create and teach lessons that address missing content that by its nature aligns with the evidence for natural selection and evolution.

Guiding Students to Examine Evolution Itself

5

Y ou've guided your students through lessons focused on the first two essential features of inquiry. You've invested in lessons that engage their interest (essential feature #1), rather than just telling them that they must learn evolution. Your resistant theistic students realize that you want to involve them as much as they are able in studying evolution without threatening their faith. You've also guided students through lessons in which they've looked at the evidence for evolution (essential feature #2), and they understand that all of the ideas about evolution must grow out of actual data. Your resistant students realize that although you respect alternative views of origins that they may have, you require them to encounter the plethora of evidence for evolution.

Now, you're ready to focus your students on evolutionary theory itself. They're ready to move to the essential feature #3 of inquiry:

Learners formulate explanations from evidence to address scientifically oriented questions. Although similar to the previous feature, this aspect of inquiry emphasizes the path from evidence to explanation rather than the criteria for and characteristics of the evidence. Scientific explanations are based on reason. They provide causes for effects and establish relationships based on evidence and logical argument. They must be consistent with experimental and observational evidence about nature. . . .

Explanations are ways to learn about what is unfamiliar by relating what is observed to what is already known. So, explanations go beyond current knowledge and propose some new understanding. For science, this means building upon the existing knowledge base. For students, this means building new ideas upon their current understandings. In both cases, the result is proposed new knowledge. (National Research Council 2000, 26–27)

The lessons you create in this part of the unit should guide students toward a basic level of understanding of evolution. Refined understanding comes later, as students continue to sharpen their understanding in the lessons focusing on essential feature #4, as discussed in Chapter 6.

Three sample lessons are given in this chapter, and they move broadly across the territory of evolution. The first focuses on whale evolution as a clear example of the evolution of a new species. The second focuses on the evolution of antiviral-resistant HIV as an example of evolution at work around us now. The third focuses on bird evolution as a historical example of the evolution of a whole new class of organisms. The three lessons are purposefully designed to paint evolution on a big-picture level so that students can focus their attention on understanding the theory itself, including recognizing misunderstandings they have about evolution.

As you prepare to teach these lessons, check your students' level of engagement. Now is a good time to reconnect with the essential question of the unit. Assess whether students are developing their own answer to "Why can't we just skip evolution?" especially if as a class they're losing interest or if the frustration of your resistant students is mounting. Consider taking ten to fifteen minutes at the start of class to refocus the students on the essential question and listen to their thoughts now that they've had several lessons on evolution. Do they have new insight on the essential question? Are they seeing any new practical applications to the study of evolution? Is the safe environment you're creating helping some to realize that evolution isn't quite so scary as they thought it would be? For a quality discussion, have the students review their initial thoughts on the essential questions that they recorded in their notebooks, brainstorm new answers in their small groups, report their new thoughts in large group, and then complete a new reflection on the essential question in their notebooks.

Natural and Supernatural Explanations

You've worked hard to engage your resistant students in an intellectually safe environment. Hopefully, they realize both the value you place on their beliefs and the sense of the importance you place on their understanding of evolution. They may even be a little confused, hearing what they think to be mixed signals from you. In the lessons focusing on essential feature #3, you guide students to clarify their understanding as you help them distinguish natural from supernatural explanations.

Your resistant theistic students are probably experiencing a world of tensions. Their families have chosen for them to receive education in the public setting, but they also emphasize the importance of faith. These students are not in a religious school where all of the content can be aligned with their faith. They're not from families where religion plays little or no importance. They're trying to make sense of their beliefs in a public environment. Now, as they study evolution, those tensions are stretched as tightly as they probably ever will be during your students' educations.

These students face a conflict between two different worldviews as they consider the origin of life on Earth. The scientific worldview focuses on answering the question "How?" by means of natural explanations of scientific evidence. The scientific worldview can't disprove religion or God, but it won't allow supernatural explanations. Theistic worldviews answer the question "Who?" by means of faith and revelation. Theistic students are asked by their faith to believe what they can't prove, and a dependence on the logic of natural explanations goes against the call they hear to believe in what they can't see. No wonder evolution can be so upsetting to some people! Proof, evidence, and natural forces—core values of science—are antithetical to living by faith.

You can't resolve these tensions for your students, so please don't try. It's not our place as science teachers to impact students' religious beliefs, even if we're being "helpful." That's something that we must leave to their families and their spiritual leaders.

We can, though, use the study of evolution to help students deepen their understanding of the nature of science itself. How do scientists make conclusions? Upon what criteria are those conclusions made? How far can science go? Does it have limits? A study of evolution can sharpen students' understanding of science itself, and the lessons in this chapter broaden the focus of study from evolution to the bigger issues of the scientific worldview. You'll begin to distinguish natural and supernatural explanations over the next several lessons.

Natural explanations are those typical of science, focusing on the work of natural forces from the physical world around us. Natural explanations can be as simple as the weathering effect on rocks of wind and water or as complex as plate tectonics providing a mechanism of continental drift. Natural selection is a natural explanation of how advantaged offspring dominate the gene pool. Evolution is a natural explanation of how the effects of natural selection over millions of years have resulted in the spectacular diversity of life on Earth.

Supernatural explanations, on the other hand, are those offered by religions, which explain the creation of the world and the origin of life by the action of supernatural forces. As your theistic students look back into the Earth's history, they find deep meaning in the interplay of supernatural forces with the natural world. These students also believe that supernatural forces are at work right now, shaping their daily lives.

In the lessons ahead, simply begin raising the difference between natural and supernatural explanations, saving in-depth discussion for the lessons outlined in the next chapter. Help your resistant theistic students look back and forth between the two worldviews. You can't and shouldn't dictate how they resolve the differences between the two in their own thinking. That's a personal decision that they must make with the guidance of their families and spiritual mentors. As students in a public school, however, they should learn to distinguish worldviews different from their faith. In English classes, they are exposed to literature with views different from their own. In history, they see multiple perspectives provided by different historical documents. In science, they should learn how science explains evidence from the natural world with natural explanations. Specific to evolution, they should understand what the theory says, but they don't necessarily have to accept it.

The Lessons

Three sample lessons are presented in this chapter. All three focus on explanations of evidence, the third essential feature of inquiry, and each is designed to help students better understand the theory of evolution itself. Each lesson begins with the question "What does the theory of evolution say?" Repeating the question is purposeful. Keep emphasizing your goal that students have a strong understanding of what evolution does and does not cover. Make sure that they don't have misconceptions about the theory. This is important for your resistant students, especially if they come to class with objections based on creationism. Many of those objections are actually based on a misunderstanding of evolution, and you don't want them to continue tilting at false windmills.

The three sample lessons move broadly between evolution and natural selection, addressing different species. The broad movement is also purposeful. To develop student understanding of the big idea of evolution, don't dive too deeply into the details. Instead, guide students to encounter widely varying evidence from the natural world so that they can see how evolution offers a natural explanation for that data.

The lessons are sequenced so that you can progressively lay the foundation for the separation of natural and supernatural explanations. In the first lesson, continue to focus on establishing an intellectually safe environment, intervening with your resistant students only if you feel that you must to keep them engaged. In the second lesson, point out the difference in natural and supernatural explanations, but without commenting on it. In the third lesson, gently challenge students' understanding, but only to make sure that they see how natural explanations work. The distinctions you make in these lessons between natural and supernatural explanations lay the foundation for the first lesson presented in Chapter 6, a lesson specifically on the nature of science and the crucial role of natural explanations.

Explaining Whale Evolution

The first lesson extends the previous one on whale evolution, and it uses the same set of resources. Students apply their previous look at the evidence for whale evolution to an understanding of the logic of the argument that scientists use in explaining how whales evolved from terrestrial mammals. As you look at the lesson plan (Table 5.1), note how it begins and ends with the question "What does the theory of evolution say?" The students use the specific example of whale evolution to look at the theory of evolution in general. The lesson moves the students more quickly through the first two essential features than previous lessons and slows down to focus on explanation, which is essential feature #3.

Guiding this lesson successfully requires having a firm grasp on the content yourself. Before teaching the lesson, go back to the evidence for whale evolution and make sure you fully understand the key points involved in the overall argument scientists use when they present whale evolution as one of the best known examples of a new species. Keep the argument clearly in your mind while students work in their small groups; this allows you to coach them and answer any questions they raise. A clear understanding is absolutely essential during the large-group discussion, where you function as facilitator. Don't be shy at that point in the lesson about pointing out errors or bringing up missing information. If you don't, students may exit the lesson with misconceptions based on the partial understanding their peers reported. You're the content expert, and students need you to step firmly into that role at this point so that they can refine their understanding to match that of established science.

For resistant theistic students, the lesson will challenge them to keep their focus on the natural explanations provided by science. Encourage these students to hold off on their objections just a little more because you want them first to understand how science explains the evidence using natural forces, but remind them that you don't expect them to accept that whales evolved, either now or anytime later in the unit. You expect them to understand the explanations offered by the scientific worldview, but not necessarily accept those explanations as part of their own personal worldview.

Explaining Antiviral Resistance

The second lesson begins and ends, as did the first, by focusing students on their understanding of the theory of evolution itself. It takes a different tack, though, by asking students to pose questions they have about the theory. The students as a class generate a list of questions that they have, and they return to those questions at the end of the lesson to see how many answers they have developed.

The lesson content focuses on how viruses evolve to become antiviral resistant, using HIV as an example. It also asks students to develop a basic sense of how HIV itself evolved from SIV (simian immunodeficiency virus). Before teaching the lesson, identify or create a resource for your students to use to understand the evidence for HIV evolution. Following are some guidelines for developing the resource, including websites you can tap. You may decide from the start, however, not to address the issue of the evolution of HIV from SIV due to the complexity it adds to the lesson.

Guidelines for Developing a Resource for the HIV Inquiry

- As always with inquiry, the resource needs to give students actual evidence to consider, not an explanation. They will develop explanations based on this evidence.
- A good source of evidence is the homepage of scientists working on the leading edge of that field. These sites often include scientific papers the authors have written that are filled with evidence you can present to your students. Although the papers are usually too technical for secondary students, you can pull graphs, charts, and data tables for your students to consider. For HIV, Dr. Brendan Larder is a leading researcher, and I found information on him[1] at the website of the HIV Resistance Response Database Initiative (Google keywords: RDI Larder).

---

[1]www.hivrdi.org/brendan.htm.

Table 5.1   Lesson Outline for Explaining the Evidence for Whale Evolution

What Does the Theory of Evolution Say?
(Learners Engage in a Scientific Question)

Lesson Segments

- Ask the students to ponder silently the question "What does the theory of evolution say?"
- Tell students that you know that some of them disagree with the theory, but right now you just want to see if they know what it says.
- Ask them to write in their notebooks a two- or three-sentence answer to the question.
- When they're through writing, tell them to put those answers aside for now and that they'll come back to them at the end of the lesson.

Accommodations for Resistant Students

- Monitor student participation to see if any refuse the task. If you intervene, do so discretely and one-to-one, gently encouraging students by letting them know that you are not trying to change their beliefs. Remind them of points from the discussion of the unit's essential question, especially those that will be most helpful for that individual student's engagement.

Review Previous Graphic Organizers
(Learners Give Priority to Evidence)

- Instruct the students to take five minutes as a group to review the graphic organizer constructed during the previous lesson on whale evolution and the article that they used in developing it.
- Ask, "What questions do you need to ask about the evidence itself before I ask you to work with your group to explain it?" Answer any questions that will hinder the students' success in the next lesson segment.

- Monitor the groups as they work, redirecting discussions of objections back to the evidence.
- Continue your previous practice of asking students who raise objections to convert them to questions. For objections that the students won't convert, compare with the previously posted objections to see if the objection needs to be added.

- The Scientific Publications tab[2] of that website gives many research papers. In particular, consider the posters listed there, because scientific posters are designed to digest the research quickly.

- In Dr. Larder's research, I found an extensive resource on antiviral resistance at the HIV Database's page on HIV Database Review Articles[3] (Google keywords: HIV database review), entitled "Mutations in Retroviral Genes Associated with Drug Resistance." Because it appears multiple times on the site, be sure to start with the most current version of the article. It will give you table after table listing the evidence for antiviral resistance in HIV, including in many cases the actual codon change occurring. You'll probably only present a few of these tables to the students; they won't need to spend time looking at a lot of the data to get the point that mutations in HIV cause them to react differently to medications.

---

[2] www.hivrdi.org/scientific_publications.htm.

[3] www.hiv.lanl.gov/content/sequence/HIV/REVIEWS/reviews.html.

Table 5.1 *Continued*

Answering the Focus Question
(Learners Develop Explanations Based on Evidence)

Lesson Segments

- Direct the students to the focus question "How Would Scientists Explain the Data?" Ask them to ponder the question silently.
- Ask a few students to give their answers, expecting that some will say simply, "Whales evolved." Use that as an opportunity to ask for a deeper answer, one where students have to begin laying out the separate arguments supporting the idea that whales evolved.
- Direct the students to work with their group for fifteen to twenty minutes to review the original article and prepare the speaker to report on the most important two or three arguments scientists use to explain the evidence for whale evolution.
- As the students work, monitor their progress to make sure they are on task and productive. Answer questions that the groups have, especially those communicated through the group's speaker or facilitator.

Accommodations for Resistant Students

- Make sure your resistant students realize that you're not asking, "What really happened?" in the sense of absolute truth. Instead, you're asking them to focus on how scientists explain the data within the limits of natural forces at work.
- If resistant students offer the explanation "God made whales," use the opportunity to make a quick distinction between natural and supernatural explanations. Remind them of the value you place on their beliefs, but refocus the discussion on the natural explanations required by science.

Group Presentations of Answers to the Focus Question
(Learners Evaluate Their Explanations)

- Designate an order for the speakers to follow and ask each speaker to present only one argument at a time, giving their group's most important one first. Post each new argument to the board. After each speaker presents, ask if any student has a question for that group or a comment about their point.
- Continue calling on speakers until all important arguments have been presented. Allow individual speakers to pass once all of their group's arguments have been presented. As the students report, assess their understanding of the scientific explanation for the whale data.
- Briefly add any key points that you feel the students missed. Be careful, though, not to undermine their work by giving a lecture covering the same points they just did.

- Informally assess how well theistic students are following the scientific arguments. How are they doing with understanding evolution but not necessarily accepting it? Do they feel safe engaging in the study without feeling that their faith is threatened?

Small-Group and Individual Metacognition
(Learners Communicate and Justify Their Explanations)

- Ask the students to silently review the answer they wrote at the beginning of the lesson to the question "What does the theory of evolution say?"
- Tell them to think about how their answers to that question changed, if at all, during the lesson.
- Ask them to write one or two sentences on how their answers changed. If their ideas didn't change, direct them to write about why they think their ideas stayed the same.
- Ask several students who are willing to read what they wrote about how their ideas did or didn't change.

- Assess how well your resistant students are building their understanding of the basics of evolutionary theory. Do some of them reorganize their understanding to correct misconceptions about evolution that they've heard from other sources? Are some of them less fearful about studying evolution because they realize that it's not the threat to their beliefs that they had originally thought?

- Consider how much to scaffold the students' work with the evidence for antiviral resistance. High school students who are adept at looking at data could probably plunge right into the tables. Middle school students and students unfamiliar with inquiry may need from you a set of step-by-step instructions guiding them in making sense of the data.

- Consider your students' prior knowledge about DNA and mutations. You may need to give students an overview of DNA codons and how they dictate cellular function, but keep this brief. Don't feel that you have to teach a three-day miniunit on DNA for students to get the point of the data.

- Web pages with scientific references can also be good sources of evidence. I found a page[4] entitled "The Origin of AIDS and HIV and the First Cases of AIDS" (Google keywords: origin HIV avert) at the Avert .org website. The advocacy stance of the Avert organization may make it a resource that you wouldn't direct your students to, but the HIV origins page lists several scientific papers that you could scan for evidence.

- The most helpful resource I found on HIV evolution was the 1999 article from *Nature* authored by Gao et al., listed as the first reference on the above Avert.org Web page. The figures in that article provide phylogenetic trees detailing how mutations in the SIV virus caused changes that allowed it to jump species and infect humans in the new form of HIV. The data in the article are technical; you'll need to scaffold for your students. Remember, it's still inquiry if you give them steps to follow in understanding the evidence.

Because HIV is sexually transmitted, you may decide that you need to use a different virus so that you don't create so much classroom controversy that the students miss the point of the lesson. Taking on evolution and HIV may just be too much for some students! Middle schoolers in general may not be able to handle a discussion of HIV. Some students come from homes and faiths that may make discussing a sexually transmitted disease truly uncomfortable because of the conflict in moral values that they may project on the discussion. Consider influenza as an alternative if you think that HIV is too much of a hot button for your students.

---

[4]http://www.avert.org/origin-aids-hiv.htm.

As you review the lesson outline presented in Table 5.2, note that some students might object, saying that what you're referring to as the evolution of HIV resistance is nothing more than natural selection. They are correct that this is an example of natural selection. As antivirals are applied to a virus population, all of the individuals without resistance are selected out, leaving only the few with advantageous genetic differences enabling them to survive. They are incorrect, though, in thinking that natural selection doesn't imply evolution. Many students view natural selection as something fundamentally different than evolution; they do not see evolution over eons as the sum of natural selection acting day by day. If students raise this point, accept their point without much comment, other than something simple like, "Oh, you see natural selection and evolution as different explanations." Keep in mind the foundational nature of these current lessons; you'll have other opportunities in future lessons to return to this point. Keep the focus on laying down the evidentiary basis they need for understanding evolution.

This lesson provides you with the opportunity to assess the comfort level of resistant students now that the unit is well under way. You've worked hard to develop a classroom climate of intellectual safety, but resistant students may still be aloof or antagonistic. Perhaps they're engaging as much as they are able and you're seeing realistic expectations for how comfortable they'll ever be during the unit. Continue asking them to understand, but not necessarily accept, evolution, whether doing so is ever comfortable for them.

Explaining Bird Evolution

This lesson begins again with the question "What does the theory of evolution say?" to keep the students focused on developing a general understanding of the theory, but provides a different approach to beginning and ending the lesson, mainly as a way of maintaining the students' interest through a variety of instruction. It focuses on having the students examine the broad sweep of scientific evidence showing how modern birds evolved from dinosaurs. The point of the lesson is that students see how scientists

Table 5.2 Lesson Outline for Explaining Antiviral-Resistant HIV

What Does the Theory of Evolution Say?
(Learners Engage in a Scientific Question)

Lesson Segments

- Ask the students to ponder silently the question "What does the theory of evolution say?"
- Ask them to think about questions they have about the theory of evolution. Emphasize again that for now, you want them to focus on what the theory says, not so much on objections they may or may not have with the theory.
- Guide a large-group discussion in which students brainstorm questions about the theory; post their questions to the board.
- Ask them to write in their notebooks one to three questions about evolution that they find most important or interesting, using either questions posted to the board or ones they've thought of on their own. As they write, move around the room to get a sense of the questions noted as important by many of your students.

Accommodations for Resistant Students

- Monitor the participation of resistant students. Gauge how comfortable they appear to feel about stating their questions. Draw their questions out if you think you can do so without starting controversy. Help them understand that you truly welcome their honest questions.
- Assess the level of intellectual safety your resistant theistic students feel about asking difficult questions. Be realistic with yourself, though. Recognize that students may feel a level of peer pressure from students of their faith that nothing you do can alleviate.
- As you monitor all students' written responses, make special note of any patterns that you see in the questions that your resistant students list as most important to them.

Examining Antiviral Resistance
(Learners Give Priority to Evidence)

- Introduce the inquiry and the resource you've chosen to guide students in understanding antiviral resistance. Clarify that they are looking at actual evidence, even though this evidence is at the level of changes within a large population, not changes to specific individuals.
- Direct them to consider two questions as they look at the evidence: How does HIV become resistant to an antiviral? What is the origin of HIV? Give them specific instructions on how to work as a group to examine the resource and to record the evidence they encounter.
- Remind them to look now for evidence and that explanations come later.

- Monitor the engagement of resistant students. If they raise objections because they sense the evolutionary implication of the lesson, encourage them for now to stick with just getting a good understanding of the evidence itself.

---

construct an argument for the evolution of a whole new class of organism, in this case birds evolving from dinosaurs, based on fossil evidence.

You'll need to develop the actual inquiry you want your students to complete. Following is a set of guidelines to help you develop your inquiry.

Guidelines for Developing the Inquiry on Bird Evolution

- Consider how directive you want to be with the instructions that you create for your students. If you teach younger middle school students or students inexperienced with inquiry, create a set of explicit, step-by-step instructions for them to follow. If your students are older or if they have had enough inquiry experience so that they can direct

Table 5.2 *Continued*

Answering the Focus Question
(Learners Develop Explanations Based on Evidence)

Lesson Segments

- Direct the students to the focus question "How can evolution explain the evidence for antiviral resistance?" Ask them to ponder the question silently.
- Direct the students to work with their group for five to ten minutes to prepare their speaker to report the group's answer to the focus question.
- As the students work, monitor their progress to make sure they stay on task and productive. Answer questions that the group has, especially those communicated through the group's speaker or facilitator.

Accommodations for Resistant Students

- If students begin discussing alternative explanations for the data, remind the groups that the task for now is to focus on the explanation provided by evolution. Tell them, though, that they're welcome to make notes of their alternative explanations for use in later discussions.

Group Presentations of Answers to the Focus Question
(Learners Evaluate Their Explanations)

- Designate one group's speaker to go first and present the explanation developed by the group.
- After the first speaker finishes, address the rest of the speakers and say, "I'm curious to know whether your group's explanation builds on or differs from what you heard. Who would like to speak next?" Make sure that the speakers realize that you don't want them simply to restate an explanation that has already been presented.
- Continue calling on speakers until all important points of the groups' explanation have been presented, assessing the students' understanding as they present.
- Briefly add any key points that you feel the students are missing without undermining the work that they did in their groups.

- Assess how well your students are building their understanding of the basics of evolutionary theory based on classroom interactions. How comfortable are they discussing their ideas with peers? Are they willing to say the word *evolution* as they talk? How many appear to be beginning to accept the division you're proposing between natural and supernatural explanations?

Small-Group and Individual Metacognition
(Learners Communicate and Justify Their Explanations)

- Ask the students to silently review the posted list of questions they raised about evolution at the beginning of the lesson. Ask, "Which of your questions about evolution did this lesson help you begin to answer?"
- Lead a large-group discussion about how students are refining their understanding of evolution itself. Mark on the posted list questions that appear to be answered and those that still remain.

- Use your judgment to decide whether to continue the large-group discussion into a brief conversation of natural and supernatural explanations. Select a couple posted questions (or items from the list of objections) that illustrate supernatural explanations crossing into natural ones. Don't attempt to completely clear up the distinction yet, but simply raise it as an issue.

themselves in pursuing answers to a question, you may simply give them oral instructions about the type of work to do and then ask them to work with their group to plan their inquiry before they start.

- Focus the students on actual scientific evidence for the evolution of birds, maintaining the focus on evidence that you've kept throughout the unit. Direct them especially to sources that give fossil evidence that students can consider.

- Consider the Tree of Life[5] Web project (Google keywords: tree of life evolution) as the main source for the students' work. Using the "Containing group" link on each page, students can work backward from *Neornithes* (modern birds) along evolutionary pathway to *Dinosauria*. The Tree of Life Web interface takes a little playing with to get used to. Explore it so you get used to how it functions, and tell your students to do the same before they plunge into the actual evidence.

- Consider having the students do their work using live Web access if at all possible. If your school has a computer lab, reserve it well in advance. As I worked on understanding the relationship between modern birds and dinosaurs, I found myself clicking up and down the phylogenetic tree again and again, trying to put the relationships together in my mind. Working online was helpful in that process.

- If you can't get computer access for your students, then consider other options. You could print key pages from the Tree of Life website and present the copies to students in random order; having to reconstruct the proper sequence will help them understand the path of bird evolution. If you have a teachers' presentation station with live Internet access, consider a large-group discussion in which students ask questions of the site and you click the links as they try to build their understanding of how birds evolved.

- Consider how you want your students to represent the understanding they're building as they examine the evidence. Is simply taking notes enough? Do you want your high school students to create a phylogenetic tree from scratch? Do you want your middle school students to finish a phylogenetic tree that you partially completed?

- Consider how to direct students to ground the explanation that they build in actual evidence. Perhaps require them to include a brief description of the key fossil evidence and age for five to ten actual species that illustrate the development of modern birds from dinosaurs. The Tree of Life pages often provide an "Information on the Internet" section that students could tap as they research specific species.

---

[5]www.tolweb.org.

- Consider how directive you want to be regarding the key relationships you want students to see as they work. An example of one such relationship would be how modifications to the wrist joint in *Maniraptora* allowed for the evolution of bird wings.[6] Based on your students' maturity, skills for inquiry, and engagement in the topic, you may decide to see if they pick up on this relationship themselves, knowing that if they miss it you can bring it out during large-group discussion later. Or, you may decide to create an explicit instruction step asking them to look at key relationships, such as wrist modifications in *Maniraptora*, that influenced bird evolution.

The lesson outline in Table 5.3 is structured similarly to previous lessons: Student work in groups to examine evidence for bird evolution and to develop their understanding of the scientific explanation of that evidence. They then provide via the group's speaker the initial points for a large-group discussion in which you guide all of the students to develop their understanding of how scientists explain the data. Note, though, that this lesson doesn't use a formal focus question. As students become more comfortable with inquiry, I prefer to shift large-group discussions to ones that are more open-ended. I want my students to own the discussions more and more, and I find that tight scaffolding can get in the way of that ownership once the students become accustomed to the basics of productive large-group discussions. If your students aren't ready for this amount of freedom, however, feel free to adjust the lesson by developing and posting a focus question to guide their small- and large-group work.

The content of this lesson is ripe for objections, and even nonresistant students may join in the dissent. The evolution of birds from dinosaurs requires interpretation of fossil evidence representing millions of years of change, and the scientific explanation seems to defy common sense. We look around us and never see one species turning into another, much less becoming a whole new class of organism, and yet this is exactly the scientific conclusion when the time span expands to millions of years. This difficulty

---

[6]See www.ucmp.berkeley.edu/diapsids/saurischia/maniraptora.html for more information.

Table 5.3 Lesson Outline for Explaining Bird Evolution

What Does the Theory of Evolution Say?
(Learners Engage in a Scientific Question)

Lesson Segments

- Ask the students to ponder silently the question "What does the theory of evolution say?" and how their answers to the question are shifting.
- Tell them that in this lesson you're going to use one of the objections people often raise to evolution as a way to further delineate what the theory actually says.
- Describe briefly the common objection that evolution can't be accurate because we don't see the evolution of new species occurring around us right now. Use several specific examples of the objection, such as monkeys becoming humans. Ask, "Does the theory of evolution say that we should see that kind of evolution occurring around us?"
- Listen to several students' responses to see how effective the objection is for engaging the students in the lesson.

Accommodations for Resistant Students

- Monitor the engagement of your resistant students. How do they respond to your raising a common objection that they probably have heard often? Do they sense that you're trying to set a trap for them or that you're maintaining an intellectually safe environment?

Examining the Evidence for Bird Evolution
(Learners Give Priority to Evidence)

- Direct the students in starting the bird inquiry that you've developed.

- Monitor the engagement of resistant students. How well are they able to examine the evidence without immediately raising objections?

Explaining Bird Evolution: Small-Group Discussion
(Learners Develop Explanations Based on Evidence)

- When the groups have had sufficient time to examine the evidence, direct them to prepare their speakers to report why birds have survived and dinosaurs have not.

- Expect objections here, especially ones along the lines of "That's just crazy. Who would believe that dinosaurs become birds?" If you've created an intellectually safe environment, students may be even more apt to express objections, but the objections should be less an attack and more an expression of their current understandings.

Explaining Bird Evolution: Large-Group Discussion
(Learners Evaluate Their Explanations)

- Call the students back together. Ask several speakers to report their group's understanding.
- After each group presents, ask the whole class for questions, comments, or concerns that they want to address. Redirect the conversation as often as needed back to the focus on natural explanations of evidence for the evolution of birds.
- Provide any expert feedback, based on your assessment of how well the students are building an understanding of the basic ideas of the evolution of new kinds of life.

- Use expressed objections as another opportunity to distinguish natural from supernatural explanations. Consider responding to objections with something similar to "I hear your concern, but I want to challenge you a little. How would you explain this evidence if you couldn't use the supernatural in your explanation? That's the challenge scientists face, even if they personally believe in the supernatural."

Small-Group and Individual Metacognition
(Learners Communicate and Justify Their Explanations)

- Ask the students, "So, what does the theory of evolution say?" Remind them how this question led off the last three lessons. Ask them to ponder silently how their understanding has changed.
- Ask the groups to work together for ten minutes to develop a two- to three-sentence statement of what the theory says, using their own words.
- Ask the speakers to read their statements for the whole class. Ask the other students to simply listen without commenting. Assess the students' understanding based on their responses, noting any refinements you'll want to target in future lessons.

- As you monitor the group work, note the engagement and understanding of your resistant theistic students. How well do they understand what evolution says? Do they realize that you expect their understanding, but not acceptance, of the theory? What are they concerned about now? Note any adjustment you'll want to make in future lessons to continue to support their learning.

is why I suggest that you allow students to openly express their objections in this lesson. The questions and concerns students raise now continue to provide a segue to the lesson you will teach next on natural and supernatural explanations. You'll use their objections to further illustrate how scientists bind themselves to the use of only natural explanations as they go about their work.

Summary

As you move forward from these three lessons, consider how well your students understand the basics of evolution for explaining evidence from the natural world about how organisms adapt in the short and long term. Review the target benchmarks appropriate to your level in Tables 2.2 and 2.3. If most students have a basic understanding, then you're ready to move forward to the lessons on essential feature #4, as discussed in Chapter 6, where students will build finesse with understanding evolution and using it to explain data. If your students still struggle with the basics of evolution, consider teaching one or two more lessons about evolution itself.

Also, consider any direct support your resistant students may need, especially if you still struggle to engage them in the study or if their objections significantly hinder their understanding. Individual or small-group conferences with resistant students may be just what some of them need now, especially if you simply listen to their concerns or confusions. Knowing that you are willing to listen goes a long way toward diffusing tension with students. If you have any students taking a leadership role in objecting to evolution, consider especially a one-on-one conference with those students. Craft a true dialogue by first listening to their concerns, as you do with any struggling student, but then ask them to listen to your goal of wanting all your students, including the other resistant students, to be able to function in the real world, which requires an understanding of evolution. Challenge them to lead well, and you may even have to direct them to tone down their dissent if you feel that it is harming other students.

6

Deepening Students' Understanding and Addressing Objections

Hopefully by this point in your unit, you see some clear indications from your students on how they are formulating their individual answers to the unit essential question. All students are seeing the importance of evolution as a central scientific explanation, and they are building their skills for using the theory to explain natural phenomena around them. This is true even of your resistant theistic students, who aren't feeling pressure to accept evolution, but are beginning to grapple with the necessity of understanding it to function as citizens in a science-saturated society.

This chapter focuses on essential feature #4, the phase of inquiry where students examine any tentative explanations they've built in light of other explanations:

Learners evaluate their explanations in light of alternative explanations, particularly those reflecting scientific understanding. Evaluation, and possible elimination or revision of explanations, is one feature that distinguishes scientific from other forms of inquiry and subsequent explanations. One can ask questions such as: Does the evidence support the proposed explanation? Does the explanation adequately answer the questions? . . . Alternative explanations may be reviewed as students engage in dialogues, compare results, or check their results with those proposed by the teacher or instructional materials. An essential component of this characteristic is ensuring that . . . student explanations should ultimately be consistent with currently accepted scientific knowledge. (National Research Council 2000, 27)

Students continue to learn in this phase of inquiry, and they often encounter new evidence that you provide them. The goal in this phase of inquiry, though, is not so much for them to encounter new phenomena as it is for them to clarify their understanding of the powerful ideas of science. In the case of evolution, the students should have already developed an initial, basic understanding of how the theory of evolution explains evidence from the natural world. As they work on this feature of inquiry, they should refine their understanding of the theory of evolution itself and exit learning focused on this feature with a clear, deeper understanding of what evolution does and does not say.

This chapter differs from the previous chapters; there are fewer sample lesson plans. After an initial lesson on the scientific worldview, I guide you to develop your own lessons focused on addressing objections to evolution as a way of building students' understanding of the theory itself. Your students' needs, interests, and backgrounds are unique, however. At this point in the unit development, use your knowledge of your students' unique needs, interests, and learning challenges to create lessons tailored to help them move toward a solid understanding of evolution. With resistant theistic students, you have to deftly walk a fine line of drawing them deeper into understanding the scientific worldview while continuing to avoid threatening their beliefs about the supernatural.

Scientific Worldview

In the last chapter, you signaled students about the differences between scientific explanations and those offered by religion. Now, you'll teach a lesson that explicitly targets the differences in those understandings. Your goal, however, is not to establish religion! Your students should have no doubt at the end of this lesson that they have just been through a science lesson, not one comparing religions. Science intersects with other beliefs at many points for many people, and evolution is clearly one of those areas.

Students need to understand how that intersection can be discussed with civility and respect. They also need to see that science places limits on itself and by its very nature cannot claim an elevated status above religion.

The first lesson sets the stage for the rest of the lessons you'll create around essential feature #4 of inquiry. In this lesson, students develop their understanding of the difference between natural and supernatural explanations. At the end of the lesson, students should be able to categorize an explanation they hear for the origin of living things as either scientific or supernatural. They will use that understanding as they examine objections to evolution, a process that will help them continue to refine both their understanding of the theory of evolution and how scientific explanations differ from religious ones.

Be cautious as you explicitly discuss religion with your students. Make sure that you clearly guide them to discuss religion in general and not any one particular religion specifically. You must be clear of the charge that you're turning your science classroom into one establishing religion. On the other hand, as a science teacher, you have a responsibility to help students understand, from a scientific point of view, how science touches on other areas of human understanding. Science intersects with philosophy, history, sociology, literature, and many other human endeavors. As science teachers, we shouldn't shy away from those intersections, including ones with religion, but we must approach them focused on helping our students better understand science itself.

The sample lesson in Table 6.1 has a different feel than previous lessons. It asks students to take a step back from a close examination of scientific evidence and look at scientific explanations from a global perspective. The lesson is still inquiry based, however. The students build explanations for the nature of science. To do this, as in all inquiry, students need evidence, and they'll use as evidence the explanations they've developed throughout the unit thus far. With this evidence, students try to explain the nature of scientific explanations, especially as those contrast with religious explanations.

Note that you will have to guide these discussions with a deft, or possibly even firm, hand at times. Students must understand that this lesson is not about belittling anyone, including people who believe religious explanations for life, those who don't, or those who believe that science offers the only valid explanation for life on Earth. Establish and maintain zero tolerance for disrespectful comments. Your role here contrasts with the "guide on the side" role often spoken of as the proper role for teachers in the inquiry classroom. At this point, you need to step clearly to center stage and directly orchestrate the discussion. This is one way you ensure that students' explanations match those of "accepted science," as mentioned in the description of essential feature #4.

Note that the lesson requires that you identify and prepare in advance an expert source for your students to consider regarding the nature of scientific explanations. The lesson focuses on students proposing and refining their definitions of natural and supernatural explanations for modern life-forms. Although essential feature #3 requires that learners begin the process of developing explanations, essential feature #4 requires that they assess their explanations against those of accepted science. It's not inquiry if students are developing explanations that are wrong scientifically! Select a brief expert source for your students to review that will help them check their understanding of scientific explanations. Probably, this will be a reading of some type, either from your textbook or an appropriate Web page. Table 2.1 from this book might be appropriate, or you could use the "Explaining Evolution" *Atlas* map[1] (Google keywords: explaining evolution Atlas) that Table 2.1 was distilled from. You may even find an appropriate source of information that is not text based, such as a video from YouTube or one you already have on hand.

Plan how you use the exit slips meaningfully and in a way that clearly communicates to student how you've honored and built on their responses. The goal of the exit slips is to help students see that although some scientists attack religion, science itself can never do so. Science restricts itself to natural explanations, so it can say nothing about the validity or deficiencies of supernatural explanations. This distinction should help your resistant students who feel that science is out to attack their faith. If you feel adept with on-the-fly discussions, you could begin the next day's lessons with student volunteers reading their exit slip responses and guiding a discussion on the inability of science to disparage religion. Even though I'm pretty

---

[1] www.project2061.org/publications/atlas/sample/a2ch10.pdf.

Table 6.1   Understanding the Scientific Worldview

Examining the Focus Question
(Learners Engage in a Scientific Question)

Lesson Segments	Accommodations for Resistant Students
■ Ask the students to think silently about the focus question "What's the difference between natural and supernatural explanations?" Post the question to the board. ■ Ask a few students to get the class started with their initial thinking about the question. ■ Clarify the question by stating, "I'd particularly be interested in your thoughts about the difference as it would be used to explain how life around us got here." ■ Continue the large-group discussion, posting students' ideas to a T-chart divided into columns for natural and supernatural explanations. ■ Some students may need you to clarify for them what you mean by *natural* and *supernatural*. Be prepared with a clarification that helps them move forward, such as, "By *natural*, I mean the natural forces of the physical world," but not one that totally gives away the distinction between scientific and religious explanations.	■ Throughout the lesson, be ready to intervene if students begin to talk disparagingly about others' beliefs. Require them to speak respectfully about theistic views, even if they hold to a different religion or no religion at all. ■ Throughout the lesson, be ready to intervene if theistic students use the discussion to proselytize about their own faith.

Examining Prior Explanations
(Learners Give Priority to Evidence)

■ Direct students to take five minutes to review their work in this unit, especially as found in their notebooks, for additional natural or supernatural explanations that the class may have missed. Hear them report their thoughts. ■ Probe as necessary to make sure that you have good examples in both columns. In the Supernatural column, guide the discussion to ensure that supernatural ideas come from multiple religions, especially if all of your theistic students are from the same religious group. ■ Ask for any missing explanations and add them to the T-chart. Be ready to add in key explanations they miss, especially the natural explanations summarized in Tables 2.2 and 2.3 and supernatural explanations from the posted objections raised previously.	■ Continue setting the proper boundaries that prevent religion from being either belittled or established. Redirecting to the lesson's focus question should keep the discussion on track.

Distinguishing Natural from Supernatural Explanations
(Learners Develop Explanations Based on Evidence)

■ Direct students back to the focus question. Ask them to work in groups to prepare a list of differences between the two types of explanations and to prepare their speaker to report the most important one or two differences from their list. ■ Listen to the speaker's reports, posting a summary list to the board.	■ Monitor the participation of your resistant theistic students, including the comfort level shown by their facial expressions and body language. Do they appear to think that religion itself is being treated fairly by the discussion? This might be a good time for you to explicitly state how religion and science both contribute to the quality of human life and how, from a scientific perspective, neither one is more valuable.

comfortable with guiding discourse, I actually would not choose that approach. Instead, I would collect the exit slips the next day, read and sort them to understand the students' different ideas, and then plan a discus-

Table 6.1 *continued*

Defining Natural and Supernatural Explanations
(Learners Evaluate Their Explanations)

Lesson Segments

- Ask the groups to develop and write down working definitions of natural and supernatural explanations. Ask students to raise their hands when they're finished.
- When a group signals that they're finished, examine its working definitions briefly to make sure the group is on the right track. If so, give students the expert reading assignment. Instruct them to read it, discuss it, and rework their definitions, incorporating any changes they feel should made based on what they read. Then, have them post the group's final definitions to the board.
- When all groups have posted, host a scientific conference in which the class examines the posted definitions and selects the best definition of natural and supernatural explanations.
- Respond to any questions students have about the difference between natural and supernatural explanations.

Accommodations for Resistant Students

- Be prepared to gently coax out questions from your resistant students, if you can do so without embarrassing them or making them feel threatened. Questions that they raise now may signal important reorganizations of their thinking, especially confusion that they may have about science producing absolute truth.

Pondering the Value of Science and Religion
(Learners Communicate and Justify Their Explanations)

- Make sure students have connected natural explanations with those offered by science and supernatural explanations as those typically offered by religions.
- Pose the question from the exit slips: "Some scientists say that science is more valuable than religion. Based on what you learned today, is that statement a scientific explanation? Why or why not?"
- Pass out the exit slips and direct students in how to complete them (e.g., silently, for homework, or group work).

- Allow students to complete the exit slips at home so resistant students can discuss the question with family members, especially if you think their families might object to the question you've asked students to think through.

sion for the lesson I intend to teach the following day. The lesson has enough potential for conflict that I would carefully plan the questions I ask and the structure of the discussion itself.

Objections to Evolution

Now that your students have clarified their understanding of the difference between scientific and religious explanations, you're ready to teach a few selected lessons on objections to evolution. Use your best judgment in deciding which and how many lessons to teach. Addressing objections, as you can imagine, sets your class up for controversy, and you're probably reading this book because you want to avoid controversy whenever you can. By now, though, you've heard from your students the key objections they have and how those objections are impeding their understanding of evolution. You've also consistently assured your students that you will address their objections. Of all the objections covered below, teach lessons only on the ones that are significant to your students. Don't teach lessons that create objections!

The objections presented here should help you see specific examples of this book's approach in action. Again and again, say to the students, "I'm not asking you to accept some specific aspect of evolution, but I do want you to understand the evidence for evolution and how scientists explain that evidence." By blatantly stating your expectation about understanding, but not necessarily accepting, you're reiterating to your students that you affirm their beliefs, but you're also helping them build the scientific understandings that they'll need for life in public society. Constantly reminding students of your approach is especially critical as you focus on the objections that many of them raise. In effect, you're not even asking them to abandon their objections. Instead, guide them to understand the scientific side of that objection, and leave to them their final decision about what they believe.

The tables in this section give only lesson concepts, not lesson outlines. The lesson concepts are starting points to help you create lessons. Use your finesse and understanding of the specific needs, interests, and backgrounds of your students in creating lessons effective for guiding them to examine their objections. The first two tables address lessons that may take a whole class period and are inquiry based. For these objections, the students probably need to encounter evidence directly and work through the process of inquiry to appreciate the scientific perspective pertinent to those objections. The later tables deal with objections for which a minilesson or lesson segment is more appropriate. As such, I don't advise you to use an inquiry-based approach for those minilessons in order to save time.

Objections About Deep Time

Six billion years of evolution is hard for most humans to truly fathom. That's an incredibly long span of time. Students from young-Earth traditions have the additional challenge of approaching the study of evolution from a worldview telling them the Earth is only thousands, not billions, of years old. Where the scientific worldview talks about an amazingly long period of time required for cosmological evolution of the universe, then for geological evolution of the Earth, and then for biological evolution of life on Earth, many resistant students believe in an amazingly short period of supernatural creation of the universe, the Earth, and life on Earth. The conflict between the two worldviews is direct and deep.

Deep time is a key issue to understanding biological evolution because of the millions of years required for the evolution of species. (See the Appendix for more on deep time and radiometric dating.) Students who approach the fossil evidence with an assumption of a young Earth will encounter significant struggles in understanding how scientists explain the evidence with Darwin's theory. These students may even see very little use for evolution because they are absolutely convinced that the world is young, not old, and that the long periods of time required by evolution just didn't happen.

Don't push hard on the issue of deep time because of how fundamental young-Earth beliefs are to some resistant students' faith. Asking them to accept the scientific worldview of a very old Earth will, for many of them, cause significant conflict in their belief systems. For some, believing in an old Earth could actually cause them to be ostracized by their faith community; the stakes are high in this area. Instead, I would guide you toward helping them simply understand, but not accept, how scientists came to view the Earth as old enough to provide the time required for evolution to work and give us the life-forms we see today.

Table 6.2 provides an analysis of objections to evolution that are rooted in misunderstandings of or disbelief in deep time. It also gives the beginning points of two lessons that you could teach to deepen your students' understanding of evolution. The first lesson focuses on radiometric dating as the key scientific evidence of the ancient age of the Earth. The second lesson extends the previous lesson you taught on bird evolution and gives students more experiences with understanding how evolutionary biologists explain the fossil record. The two lessons actually could be taught together. Without the eons established by radiometric dating, evolution does not have the time required for the development of the species we see today.

Table 6.2   Lesson Concepts for Objections About Deep Time

Objection to Evolution	Target Scientific Understandings	Focus Question for Lesson	Resistant Students' Struggles	Key Message
"The Earth is a lot younger than scientists say. All of that carbon dating stuff can't be trusted because it gives the wrong dates." "The Earth is only six thousand years old, so there's not enough time for everything to have evolved."	Radiometric dating techniques are good science. Combined with the uniformitarianism inherent in the scientific worldview, radiometric dating of many different types continually uphold the ancient age of the Earth and of fossils.	What is radiometric dating and why do scientists trust it?	For some students, just examining radiometric dating with an open mind is a difficult struggle. Students who begin to accept scientific dating techniques may face doubts about their faith.	"I'm not asking you to accept that fossils prove life on Earth to be millions of years old. I want you to understand, however, that evolution explains well the data when we stick to the rule that science allows only natural explanations."
"No one has ever seen macroevolution really happen." "You just can't get complex life from simple life-forms."	*Macroevolution*, as creationists typically use the term, could never be observed by humans because it takes millions of years. The only way to observe macroevolution is to see it occurring across the fossil record, which shows a clear progression from simple to complex life-forms.	How does the fossil record support the idea of evolution of new classes of organisms?	Many resistant students see a direct conflict between their beliefs in special creation and the scientific view regarding evolution of new classes of organisms.	"I'm not asking you to accept that new classes of organisms came about by evolution, but I do want you to understand how natural explanations of the fossil record result in that conclusion."

Note how for each objection, the table gives the corresponding scientific understanding, a possible focus question for the lesson, possible resistant students' struggles, and a message you can use in guiding the student toward understanding, but not accepting, evolution. The other tables in this chapter will follow a similar format. The Target Scientific Understandings column gives you the science that contrasts with typical student objections. The Focus Question for Lesson column helps you think about how to focus the lesson away from controversy. The Resistant Students' Struggles column gives examples of possible struggles your students are facing, in case you're not sure why resistant students raise objections in this area. The Key Message column gives you an example of the kind of message that you can use to continue to reinforce with your resistant students how you don't want them to abandon their faith, but do want them to understand science.

Inquiry is probably your best approach for helping students understand deep time. As you've done throughout the unit, present students with evidence for an old Earth and guide them in seeing how scientists explain that evidence from natural causes at work. Don't simply tell them what they should believe. Several of the resources identified in the Deep Time and Radiometric Dating section of the Appendix should help you identify evidence you can use for building an effective inquiry. Hopefully all of your students, including your resistant ones, will see how natural causes provide a plausible explanation for the evidence. Be aware, though, that resistant students may be quite skeptical of those explanations because of their disbelief about deep time. Help them to understand the evidence for deep time, without requiring they accept that the Earth is old.

Objections Based on Misunderstandings of Evolution Itself

Evolution is hard to understand. It's complex and abstract, and it usually can't be directly observed. Resistant students can bring to the study of evolution a worldview having minor to major conflicts with the scientific worldview that modern life-forms evolved from single-celled organisms due only to natural causes. Without even trying, therefore, resistant students may enter your classroom with fundamental misunderstandings of the evidence for or the explanation of evolution. Table 6.3 follows the same format as the previous table and helps you think about how you might develop lessons that address four common objections to evolution that are rooted in misunderstandings of the theory itself.

To effectively structure inquiry in the first lesson, ask students to compare an older, incomplete fossil series with a current one in which some of the gaps are filled in. I was first introduced to this way of thinking during a talk by Eugenie Scott, Executive Director of the National Center for Science Education (www.ncseweb.org). She helped me see that gaps will always exist in the fossil record due to its very nature, but as paleontology progresses, many of those gaps will grow smaller and some will even be filled. Showing students how gaps in different fossils series have been filled over the past decades of science should help them better understand how science works. (See the Appendix section on whale evolution for related

Objection to Evolution	Target Scientific Understandings	Focus Question for Lesson	Resistant Students' Struggles	Key Message
"There are just too many missing links for evolution to be true." "If evolution is true, then we'd have a whole lot more fossils out there showing how one species became another."	The fossil record, by its very nature, will have gaps because not all life-forms fossilized. At the same time, scientists consistently see gaps getting smaller as more fossils are unearthed.	Why aren't evolutionary biologists worried by gaps in the fossil record?	Students may have heard a lot of information about gaps, especially if they're attuned to creationist arguments. Students may struggle with the idea that if a scientific theory is accepted, then the proof for that theory has to be absolutely solid.	"I don't expect you to believe that the fossil record proves life evolved on Earth, but I do want you to understand why the scientific community accepts evolution even with missing evidence."
"Don't scientists themselves disagree about whether evolution really happened?" "Evolution is just a theory."	Evolution is a bedrock, not tentative, belief of the scientific community. Scientists may disagree on evolutionary mechanisms, but not evolution itself.	Which do scientists debate: Did evolution occur or how did it occur?	Because resistant students typically see evolution as implausible, they focus on scientific examples that support their position. In everyday language, *theory* means something tentative. Students may think that "the theory of evolution" is just a guess by scientists.	"I don't expect you to accept that evolution is the way life came to be on the Earth, but I want you to understand that scientists accept that idea and go about their work as if evolution is a fact."

resources). Remember, though, your goal is not to get resistant students to accept that the fossil record provides conclusive proof that life evolved.

To answer the second focus question, ask students to look at statements from major scientific organizations and groups of scientists. Rather than telling students what scientists say about the bedrock nature of evolution, guide them to encounter for themselves the statements of multiple scientific groups. In this sense, you're still teaching by inquiry. You're starting with an engaging, scientific question, "Which do scientists debate: Did evolution occur or how did it occur?"; the evidence you're putting in front of students is the beliefs of practicing scientists. You're asking students to develop a general explanation of the importance of evolution in science. You're not, however, asking them to accept evolution, just understand that scientists go about their work as if evolution is an absolute fact.

Make sure as you teach this, and any of these lessons on objections, to guide students to connect back to the understandings they developed during the lesson on natural and supernatural explanations, described in Table 6.1. Help students deepen their understanding of natural explanations by seeing that science has limits; it can't displace religion. Also, help them to deepen their understanding by seeing that one of the key limits that scientists place on themselves is restricting their explanations to natural causes, even if they personally believe in the supernatural.

Objections Based on Beliefs

Religion has value. It has a long record of bringing beauty and hope to humanity, and spiritual people speak of how their faith makes them kinder, more helpful, more patient, and more focused on others. Religions have their own worldviews, however, and theistic students who adhere devoutly to their faith will experience conflict between the way their faith teaches them to look at the world and some of the tenets of the scientific worldview. Theistic students in public schools negotiate this conflict on multiple fronts, and the conflict is not simply science versus religion. In social science classes, they encounter theories of human behavior that conflict with their understanding of how people and society work. In English classes, they read literature that opposes their beliefs in subtle or even overt ways. In health classes, they may be taught sex education practices that conflict with their morality. They are growing up in the public, and they are learning to negotiate the intersections between their beliefs and the other worldviews they encounter.

In the life science and biology class, this negotiation continues as theistic students study evolution. Table 6.4 gives several objections that resistant students typically raise because of the very nature of having grown up in faith traditions. These objections don't show that students are stupid, ignorant, or obstinate. Instead, they show that students are thinking about the conflict and trying to make sense of their worlds.

The lessons you create for these objections probably won't require a whole period to teach. That's why the focus questions are labeled in the table as those for minilessons. You can address these objections in a short period of time, and you probably won't want to teach these lessons by inquiry.

Table 6.4   Lesson Concepts for Objections Based on Beliefs

Objection to Evolution	Target Scientific Understandings	Focus Question for Minilesson	Resistant Students' Struggles	Key Message
"Everything evolutionists say happened is really a result of Noah's flood."	Uniformitarianism is a key assumption of the scientific worldview.	What is uniformitarianism and how does it guide scientific explanations?	Students who have been taught that Noah's flood literally happened will struggle with science totally ignoring such a major event.	"I'm not asking you to doubt Noah's flood. Instead, I want you to understand how the principles of science cause a very different approach to the evidence scientists collect and how they explain what they find."
"There's just no way that life evolved. You can't get living stuff from nonliving stuff."	Because scientists are bound only to natural explanations, they seek to explain how life evolved from nonliving matter by natural means.	Why don't scientists use supernatural explanations?	The beauty and complexity of life on Earth has always been something that causes humans from many different religions to believe that forces bigger than just natural causes must be at work.	"I'm not asking you to stop believing in supernatural events like creation. I do want you to understand, however, why scientists don't use the supernatural when they explain the beginning of life on Earth."
"Isn't science a search for Truth?"	Science can never prove anything in an absolute sense. It can disprove things, but it can never establish truth absolutely.	Is science about a search for Truth?*	Absolute truth is part of the worldview of theistic students, beginning with their belief that the supernatural absolutely exists and impacts life on Earth. They are often truly surprised by any worldview, including that of science, that does not seek truth as its final product.	"I'm not asking you to give up your belief in absolute truth. I do want you to understand, however, that science is valuable even if it gives us tentative understandings."

*This question should be posted in written form so that students clearly see that by capitalizing the first letter, you're talking about truth in an absolute sense.

These topics can be addressed well through bursts of direct instruction inserted in other lessons, especially when the topic naturally comes up.

For the first objection, give students a brief overview of uniformitarianism, the scientific assumption that the natural processes at work today were the processes at work in the past. As you overview uniformitarianism, open up the discussion for questions from the students and listen to make sure that they really understand uniformitarianism and its implications for explaining the way events occurred as life on Earth evolved. Let students know also that you recognize that this scientific idea is in conflict with many spiritual beliefs. Listen to their questions and guide them to understand the implications of uniformitarianism for scientists' work.

For the second objection, be ready to talk about scientists who are spiritual people themselves, but who respect the scientific requirement that they give explanations based only on natural causes. Frances Collins, who leads the Human Genome Project, is a good example. Guide students to grasp during this minilesson that many scientists are people of faith themselves, and they don't reject their supernatural beliefs as they go about the presentation and publication of their data. They simply limit themselves to natural explanations in their work. They may even talk about their beliefs across the laboratory bench or when they're out in the field, but they don't weave their spirituality into their scientific publications.

The third objection is going to be tough for any students in grades 6–10 because so many of them see the world in absolute terms. If you teach younger students, you may even decide that addressing this objection is developmentally inappropriate for your students. Begin the minilesson by asking the students the focus question. Then engage them in a discussion of the term *absolute truth* to make sure that they understand what you mean by this; ask them to list some examples of things that they believe to be absolutely true. Then, guide them to think back through the inquiries they've conducted as your students, both in the evolution unit and in other units you've taught. Direct them to see how none of the inquiries absolutely proved anything, but they did disprove certain ideas. Again, listing specific examples on the board will help. Make sure students are getting the basic idea that science isn't in the business of absolute truth, but as you've done before, continue to reassure your resistant students that you are not trying to change their belief in absolute truth itself.

Other Objections

Tables 6.5 through 6.8 give a final set of objections that really don't fit under a single theme, but I offer some guidance in addressing these as they consistently come up when resistant students learn evolution. As with the previous set of objections, I suggest that you're prepared to teach minilessons as the issues come up, especially if you could do so on a need-to-know basis.

Students in general can come to the study of evolution with the misconception that evolution is only about competition between individuals or among species, especially if the only evolution examples they've seen address competition, not cooperation. They also typically have little experience hearing scientists talk about wonder, beauty, and awe. Theistic students, in particular, may have heard or read creationist objections around this topic. In your minilesson structured after Table 6.5, remind students of examples of evolution at work to bring good things, such as the beauty of flowers and bird plumage or the cooperation that occurs in the animal kingdom. Provide them with examples of scientific ideas that focus on the beauty of the natural world, such as the work of environmental scientists who work to preserve that beauty.

Table 6.6 is one of the few sections in this book that will get anywhere close to addressing creationism directly. By now, you've clearly seen how my approach is much different from teaching that either supports or attacks creationism. These objections often find their roots in students' knowing very little about the peer-review process required for scientific publications. They think of science as something that exists in their textbook, when science can better be thought of as the understandings of the scientific community as published in peer-reviewed journals. To teach the minilesson in Table 6.6, describe in general how a scientific article gets

Table 6.5   Lesson Concept for Objections About Beauty and Wonder

Objection to Evolution	Target Scientific Understandings	Focus Question for Minilesson	Resistant Students' Struggles	Key Message
"If everything evolved because of survival of the fittest, then why do we have anything good around us? Why is the world so beautiful?"	Evolution doesn't discount beauty; beauty can be advantageous in natural selection. Evolution shows how cooperation between organisms can provide advantage. The scientific worldview recognizes the world as a wonderful, amazing place and science as often a pursuit of beauty and awe.	Does evolution say that the world should be a harsh, even terrible, place where everything is fighting for survival?	Students who have been taught creationist objections may believe that evolution focuses only on the harsh side of competition. Students may believe that good, truth, and beauty in the world come chiefly from, or only from, their religion.	"Would it surprise you if I said, 'Scientists seek out the good and the beautiful in their work'? I'm not asking you to accept that science is better than or even equal to your religion, but I do want you to understand the value that science places on helping humans to see the wonder and beauty of living on Earth."

Table 6.6 Lesson for Key Creationist Objections

Objection to Evolution	Target Scientific Understandings	Focus Question for Minilesson	Resistant Students' Struggles	Key Message
"Fossils have been found that prove that people and dinosaurs lived at the same time." "Didn't scientists make up fake fossils to prove people evolved?" "Aren't peppered moths a fake?" "The moon has just a little bit of dust, so the Earth can't be six billion years old."	Scientific evidence and explanation must go through the rigorous process of peer review before being accepted by the scientific community.	Can we trust science?	Students who have been exposed to creationist objections may believe that some or all scientists try to deceive the public. Students may have seen evidence that in their understanding contradicts evolution.	"I'm not trying to get you to disbelieve in creation, but I do want you to understand that science has layers of rules and procedures to prevent data from being faked, bad explanations from being accepted, and a few scientists from imposing their personal beliefs on the rest of the scientific community or the public."

Table 6.7 Lesson for Objections About Complexity

Objection to Evolution	Target Scientific Understandings	Focus Question for Minilesson	Resistant Students' Struggles	Key Message
"There's no way that something as complex as the eye could have just evolved. It has too many parts."	The fossil record gives clear evidence of a development in complexity, with regard both to more complex species and to more complex structures and organs required for those species to function.	How do evolutionary biologists explain the development of complex structures?	Belief in a supernatural being who creates complex life makes much more sense to some students than belief in a universe that orders itself into the complexity and beauty we see.	"I'm not asking you to accept that complex structures evolved without supernatural intervention. I do want you to understand how scientists, bound by natural explanations, explain fossil evidence."

Table 6.8 Lesson for Objections Based on the Second Law

Objection to Evolution	Target Scientific Understandings	Focus Question for Minilesson	Resistant Students' Struggles	Key Message
"The second law of thermodynamics says that evolution couldn't happen."	The Earth is not a closed system, because of the amount of energy flowing in from the Sun, and so the second law does not apply. The second law can't be used to disprove evolution because of the tremendous amount of energy in the system after the Big Bang.	Does the second law of thermodynamics disprove evolution?	The second law of thermodynamics seems tantalizingly simple and therefore an easy tool to use to disprove evolution.	"You don't have to give up your belief that the supernatural was involved in the creation of the universe and life on Earth, but I want you to clearly understand the limitations of the second law."

published, especially how the evidence and explanation in the article is carefully scrutinized for bias and error. Explain also how science, although not infallible, is inherently self-correcting; possibly give an example such as how Peking man fossils have come to be accepted as scientific evidence even though the originals are now lost to science. Question the students to make sure they're getting the basic idea of how we know scientific explanations are carefully guarded against bias, but also help resistant students understand that you're not trying to get them to give up their beliefs in special creation.

One problem with evolution for the general public is how it is counterintuitive at times. For many people, it's truly hard to believe that the amazing complexity of the world around us resulted simply from the impersonal plus time plus chance, as the Christian philosopher Francis Schaeffer has said. For resistant theistic students, the idea that complexity just happened is usually ludicrous to them because of their prior belief that supernatural forces are at work. When this objection comes up, be prepared per Table 6.7 to point the students to the fossil record, which clearly shows that complex organisms did evolve. Of course, students may quickly say, "But God made that happen." As you have done with their other objections, remind them that you don't want to change their beliefs, but that you do want them to understand how scientists develop clear explanations of the development of complex organisms using only natural explanations.

Table 6.8 addresses the very specific, but common, objection based on the second law of thermodynamics. This one always makes me chuckle a little because of how students and adults who would normally say, "Gosh, I don't know a thing about physics," can be quick to invoke this very deep and profound law of physics in casual conversations. Your minilesson should be targeted chiefly on helping students see how the second law simply does not disprove evolution. On the surface, when used simplistically, it does, but when students really understand what the second law means, they will see that evolution is allowed under it. Help your resistant students see throughout the discussion, however, that you're not trying to take away their belief in creation. You just don't want them defending their beliefs with scientific misunderstandings.

Summary

Go back and review your final focus for the unit and make sure that you've given your students the opportunity to learn all of the big ideas. Tables 2.4 and 2.5 give my final focus, and as you look at those, note how the lessons cover the big ideas of the scientific worldview, biological evolution, and natural selection. Your students will still have some final opportunities to refine their understandings as you address essential feature #5; the next chapter will guide you to allow your students to pursue their own question using project-based learning. Therefore, make a final assessment to see if you need to teach any additional lessons or minilessons to the whole class, while they're still all together, to ensure that your students understand the main concepts of evolution.

Also, do a final assessment of the engagement level of your resistant students. You've been working through weeks of lessons to engage them and to communicate to them how you value both their beliefs and an understanding of evolution. You've respectfully listened to their objections and developed lessons helping them to see scientific answers to those objections. If they're not engaged now or if they're still highly threatened by evolution, perhaps you've done all that you can. You may need to take the pressure off yourself to accomplish much more with them in the unit. You've planted a few seeds of scientific understanding that may sprout and take root later on in these students' lives.

7

Using Project–Based Learning to Solidify Student Understanding

Your evolution unit is drawing to a close. Students are engaged. They can articulate answers to the essential question "Why can't we just skip evolution?"—answers both for society in general and for themselves personally. Resistant students also can articulate answers to the question. They see how evolution intersects their lives, but they also know now that you are giving them freedom to come to their own conclusions about what they believe about evolution itself.

Your students see the evidence for evolution. They've seen multiple examples of evolution at work in many different species. Resistant students may not accept that evolution occurred, but they see clearly the evidentiary base that scientists draw on. Your students can use the theory of evolution to explain evidence, both over short periods of time when natural selection works to select individuals within a population better fit to survive and over eons when natural selection works so that new species emerge and others go extinct.

Your students also understand better the nature of science itself due to their study of evolution. They know science limits itself to natural explanations, and they can distinguish natural and supernatural explanations. Your theistic students see more clearly that science by its own rules can't play a trump and claim superior explanations over their beliefs, and students see that people of faith have a clear place in the scientific community as long as they're willing to limit themselves to natural explanations as they publish their findings.

As you look back at the target benchmarks in Tables 2.1, 2.2, and 2.3, you have confidence that most of your students have general understandings in place. You still want them to refine their understanding, though. They're not through with their learning about evolution. Hence the need for this final unit and student work on the final essential feature of inquiry.

> *Learners communicate and justify their proposed explanations.* Scientists communicate their explanations in such a way that their results can be reproduced. This requires clear articulation of the question, procedures, evidence, proposed explanation, and review of alternative explanations . . . Having students share their explanations provides others the opportunity to ask questions, examine evidence, identify faulty reasoning, point out statements that go beyond the evidence, and suggest alternative explanations for the same observations. Sharing explanations can bring into question or fortify the connections students have made among the evidence, existing scientific knowledge, and their proposed explanations. (National Research Council 2000, 27)

Essential feature #5 requires that, just as scientists finalize their research into a presentation for a conference or a paper for a journal, so your students need to finalize their understandings in front of others. Just as scientists often have to retool or refine their explanations, based on their interactions with their peers, so too will your students have to refine their understandings when they present their findings. Just as scientists have to carefully organize their findings when they attempt to publish them, so too will your students have to carefully organize their understandings when they go before review by a broader audience. And, throughout all this work, your students keep learning about evolution, resolving old questions and asking new ones, just as scientists deepen their understanding of their inquiry as they prepare it for review.

My philosophy on essential feature #5 is probably a little different than that of many science teachers. On first blush, essential feature #5 sounds like a call for traditional lab reports. I take a project-based approach to meeting this final essential feature, however. I've found that teaching students how to do lab reports well is tedious and deadly boring for most students. Occasional lab reports are good for students, but a steady diet of them is not the best way to fulfill essential feature #5.

Instead, project-based learning can accomplish this final feature, especially because students can connect the content of the unit with the lives they live every day. The 4MAT model of instruction developed by Bernice McCarthy (2000) calls for a final quadrant of instruction in which learners take the content and find out how it applies directly in their lives. I create projects that students can accomplish only when they see how the content, in this case evolution, helps them better understand their world. This approach also helps me achieve the call for science literacy in the national science standards. Students are scientifically literate (Rutherford and Ahlgren 1990) with regard to evolution if they understand the big ideas of evolution and can use evolution as a powerful explanatory system, even if they don't accept evolution itself.

With all that in mind, you're now ready to sharpen the unit essential question for your students to require them to find personal, not large-group, answers to "Why can't we just skip evolution?" If students work on their culminating projects in small groups, then the "we" in the essential question becomes the students in the small group as they seek an answer that makes sense to the members of the group. If your students work individually on their projects, then the question driving their projects becomes "Why can't I just skip evolution?"

Possible Projects

Most of the rest of this chapter focuses on possible projects to help students finalize their understanding of evolution and its value in their everyday lives. The projects are not intended to be an exhaustive list. Instead, they are examples designed to stir your thinking about projects you could create that match well the needs and interests of your students. The first set of projects is designed for all students. Any of your students, including your resistant students, might select one of these projects. The second set of projects is designed to meet the needs of resistant theistic students, although nontheistic students might select one of these. Following the description of the projects, I give a few guidelines on how to implement project-based learning in this unit. I also give a quick overview of some other approaches to essential feature #5 that aren't project based.

For All Students

Table 7.1 overviews a set of projects appropriate for all students. The project topics are evolution in popular media, solving practical problems, understanding the local controversy, and a student-generated project. The rest of the information in the table should help you think through how to present to project and the end result that defines quality work on the project. The Introducing the Project column notes how you might present the project idea to your students on the day you kick off the projects with the whole class. The Possible Product column gives possible submission forms for the

Table 7.1   Projects Appropriate for All Students

Project Focus	Introducing the Project	Possible Product	Excellence Standard	Learning Standard
Evolution in popular media	Give one example you've found and explain how people can misunderstand popular media if they don't understand evolution.	Pamphlet/Web page combination	Reviewers are motivated to inform themselves about evolution, especially because of the compelling examples selected.	Students document their increased understanding of evolution as they research the science behind media examples.
Solving practical problems	Present two to three societal problems requiring an understanding of evolution.	Email/YouTube video	Reviewers recognize how lack of knowledge about evolution hinders understanding of important problems and see clear steps they can take to increase their knowledge about evolution.	Students document their increased understanding of evolution as they research the science behind potential societal problems.
Understanding the local controversy	Read local examples of controversy about evolution, such as emails you've received or letters to your local paper's editor.	Role-play or drama Case studies with resources	Each student clearly identifies ways that she or he can better understand people from the community who believe differently about evolution.	Students document their increased understanding of evolution as they seek to craft answers to the controversy.
Student-selected project	You've heard project examples that I've thought of. Has anyone thought of another project idea that you might like to pursue? I'm open to other options.	Students propose as part of their project plan a final form appropriate to the nature of their project.	Students negotiate with you an excellence standard and an overall project plan before they begin actual work on the project.	Students propose as part of their project plan how they will document their increased understanding of evolution.

project, and the Excellence Standard column describes a relevant standard that you could use to hold the students responsible for high-quality work.

The final column needs a more extensive explanation. I don't like assigning projects that turn into fluff work. In my classroom and many others, I've seen projects stray from the science content so much that they merely become art projects at best and often just busywork. Those projects are disappointing and show little or no evidence that students understand the science content any more than they did before they started the project. That's why I like to implement a learning standard, as given in the final column of the table. As you scan through that column, note that I envision projects for this unit that allow students to continue learning about evolution itself as they complete the project. This element should be a major component of the scoring rubric for the project. Students shouldn't score well on the project if they don't clearly show how they have increased their scientific understandings.

Evolution appears consistently in popular media, and average citizens who don't understand evolution may miss important information. An example of this would be the movie *Jurassic Park.* How much of the science eluded audience members, or even worse, how much of the science fiction in the movie did viewers think to be actual fact? In the first project, students create a guide to help others see why they need to know the basics of evolution to understand it when it comes up in popular culture. Students who select this project find examples of evolution in popular media and document how ignorance of evolution hinders people from engaging well with popular culture. They will probably also find clear examples where misunderstandings of evolution are actually presented by popular culture. An excellent presentation of this project could be accomplished via a two-stage persuasive piece aimed at fellow students and adults in their community. The first stage captures the attention of their target audience, for example, with a flyer that they can distribute by hand or with a creative email that they can distribute broadly. The first-stage communication gets some of the target audience to review the second-stage materials, where the students actually present their case for the need to understand evolution. The second stage works well as a Web page, a video (possibly delivered via YouTube), or more written information. The second stage should report many examples from the students' research of the necessity of understanding evolution. Students are evaluated on how well they conduct their research, how effectively they communicate their message to the target audience, and how they have continued to learn about evolution itself during the project. Continued learning about evolution in this project flows naturally out of the students' need to understand the science behind the popular media examples they choose as they focus on educating their audience.

Evolution is essential to understanding and finding solutions to practical problems around us. An obvious current example is the threats caused by climate change to the survival of many species, especially because evolution correctly explains how slowly most species adapt to climate change. Other practical problems for which an understanding of evolution is required include antibiotic resistance, chemotherapy, and agricultural techniques. In the second project, students focus on helping their target audience commit themselves to better understanding evolution so that they can use it in understanding real-world problems they face.

Students will select and research several practical problems that require an understanding of evolution in order to create solutions. They then develop a two-stage communication similar to that of the first project. The first stage of communication, such as a flyer or an email, creates interest among the target audience for reviewing the information in the second stage, a more detailed communication, which could be in a document, a pamphlet, or video delivered over the Internet. Students choosing this project are evaluated on the quality of their work in planning the overall project, conducting research, creating both stages of their message, and learning more about evolution as they go. Continued student learning about evolution in this project flows naturally out of the students' need to understand the practical problems they select in depth so that they can both capture their audience members' attention and educate them on the pertinent science.

The third project may be one that interests students who are not theistic themselves, but see how difficult evolution is for many of their friends. It may also be a project that a team of theistic and nontheistic students undertake to better understand the way evolution creates conflict in a community. This project takes a local focus and asks students to put on a journalism or anthropology hat as they find out more about the understandings, beliefs, and feelings of people in their community about evolution, including both those who take a strong stand for and those who take a strong stand against evolution. Help the students understand that their job is not to solve the controversy, but simply to understand the perspectives of those involved in local controversy. Their product would focus on presenting the perspectives of the people they interview with dignity and respect, no matter the position of the people they are portraying. Students could create the script for a short drama that depicts the perspectives of the people involved, or students could write up case studies of the key people involved and present resources that help with understanding each person's perspective. Students' work on the project would be evaluated on the quality of their planning of the overall project, conducting the research in such a way that the people they talk with feel respected, presenting their new understandings in a way that dignifies everyone involved, and learning more about evolution as they go. Continued student learning in this project flows naturally out of students' need to understand better the scientific questions or concerns raised by the people they interview.

The fourth project is for those students who have a million great ideas and learn best when they get to pursue one of those ideas. Most of my students typically do not take this option; they're happy to pursue one of the standard options I've laid out. But as I go over project options with my students, I usually see one or two whose mental wheels really start spinning. They're thinking of ideas that I never would have come up with. Some of the ideas are wacky or unrealistic, but some of them are really good. If students are willing to do the work of negotiating a good plan with me in advance of starting their work, I let them pursue their own ideas. I make them do the work of negotiating, though, by requiring them to put their thoughts down in writing so that I can review them during a quite moment and have a record of the work that they're doing. They're free to modify their project plan as they work, but they must make any changes in writing as well.

For Theistic Students

Table 7.2 presents a set of projects designed to meet the needs of theistic students as they continue to deepen their understanding of evolution while

Table 7.2   Projects Targeting the Needs of Theistic Students

Project Focus	Introducing the Project	Possible Product	Excellence Standard	Learning Standard
Finding a mentor	"Some of you are struggling because you like science, but you see conflict with your faith. It might help you to find a scientist of your faith that you could talk to."	Lessons learned from my mentor Survival guide and project tips for future students	Students develop and execute a sensible plan for finding a mentor from their faith, including what they learn from any mentors they find.	Students identify two or three of their most important remaining questions about evolution at the beginning of the project and document their progress on better understanding, but not necessarily accepting, the scientific answers to those questions.
Family guide to answering the essential question	"I know that some of your families are skeptical of evolution. Consider helping your family develop their own answer to the essential question."	Family discussion guide Extended family pamphlet*	The project shows good potential for motivating students' family members to engage in learning more about evolution and developing a familywide answer to the essential question.	After interviewing family members to understand their questions about evolution, students document their progress on finding scientific answers to questions not addressed previously in the unit.
Personal answers to essential question	"I know that this unit has touched on some of your deeply held beliefs, and I want you to have the opportunity to make more sense of that."	Post hoc journal entries Synthetic reflections on interviews of religious leaders and scientists Survival guide for future theistic students	The project shows that the student has phrased for him- or herself a clear and compelling answer to the unit essential question.	Students identify two or three of their most important remaining questions about evolution at the beginning of the project and document their progress on understanding, but not necessarily accepting, the scientific answers to those questions.
Student-selected project	"You've heard examples of projects that I've thought of. I'm open to other options, either ones that you want to mention now or talk with me about later."	Students propose as part of their project plan a final form appropriate to the project.	Students negotiate with you an excellence standard and an overall project plan before they begin actual work on the project.	Students propose as part of their project plan how they will document their increased understanding of evolution.

*This product could probably be converted to a guide for the use with the students' faith congregation.

staying true to the faith of their families. Theistic students won't be required to work on these projects. You'll only present them as options so that your theistic students know that they are free to follow a personal pathway that is important to them, maybe even one that strengthens their faith, if they would like to. You're not establishing religion in your classroom, however. You're holding your theistic students to the same levels of quality as the other students, you're requiring them also to continue learning about evolution as they work, and most important, you're not advocating any one faith in your instruction.

The first project is probably the most beneficial for theistic students, but also the hardest to accomplish. Its benefit lies in the power of mentors. Theistic students who love science can often feel alone. They look for evidence, but they live in spiritual communities often telling them to believe without evidence. They believe in the supernatural, but they love a subject that limits its talk to only natural causes. Mentors ease these feelings of isolation because the student then is able to see a role model who both believes and loves science. This project is difficult, though, because mentors can be difficult to find. To accommodate for this difficulty, the excellence standard focuses mostly on students executing a good plan for finding a mentor, not on whether they actually find one or not. Students who select this project may need help from you if they run into dead ends. Encourage them to network by asking around in their faith community for suggestions of possible mentors. Suggest tips for making contact with a mentor, such as establishing contact through email, explaining what they're doing and why, making a request for a phone interview limited in time, and how to follow up on the phone interview. You might require students who select this project to document the work they do, especially in case they run into a total dead end and are unsuccessful in finding a mentor. They should still get full credit on the project as long as they've searched thoroughly. If they are successful, their product should focus on what they learned from their mentor and how the experience has impacted them. If they aren't successful, they might produce some kind of tip sheet for future students sharing the lessons they learned (assuming that in the years ahead, you'll have future students from the same faith community in your classes, and if you keep these tips sheets on file, they can start with these lessons learned and hopefully be more successful with their searches).

Families can be key support for theistic students, even at times quietly shielding science-oriented students from members of their faith community who disapprove of science. The second project for theistic students focuses on students helping their families better understand evolution, which might even have a positive ripple effect into their faith communities.

Students who select this project will create a discussion guide for their nuclear family and a pamphlet for their extended family. To prepare the discussion guide, students will interview family members to understand their questions and concerns about evolution, conduct research to find answers to those question and to deepen their own understanding of evolution, and then compile their findings in such a way that it is a productive tool for their family to use in beginning to talk about evolution. Students are evaluated on how well they research both their family's questions and evolution, how well their final product appears to work in starting a productive discussion about evolution, and whether they've deepened their own understanding of evolution.

Some of your theistic students may do some highly personal work as they seek to solidify their understanding of evolution. They may feel threatened by the study or awkward talking about their new understandings at home or around people of their faith. The third project allows students to craft their own personal answer to the unit essential question in a form that they feel comfortable with. Their task is to pursue their own answer to the essential question, documenting well the research that they have done and the new understandings that they come to. Some highly reflective students may create a journal in which they write entries that they might have made in a journal throughout the unit. They would solidify their own answer to the essential question as they reflect on the feelings, questions, and new understandings that they experienced throughout the unit. Some highly interactive students may interview leaders in their faith communities and scientists about their views of the importance of evolution as a way to gain more insight on the essential question. They would finalize their understandings into a report in which they use what they've learned in interviews to come to their own conclusions. Students who are concerned about future resistant students and their struggles with learning evolution could create a survival guide for those future students. As your students think about how they would coach future students on navigating the evolution unit, they will need to clarify their own answer to the essential question, using that understanding as the central idea of their survival guide. Students would be evaluated on the quality of work that they do in creating and executing a project plan; in the research work they do, including strengthening their understanding of evolution itself; and in showing the clarity of understanding of the essential question that they come to, as represented in the product of their project.

The fourth option here follows the last option given in the section for all students. Theistic students who have a good idea that you haven't mentioned can pursue their ideas, as long as they do the work required to negotiate with you each step of the project before they do it.

Guiding the Projects

I'm not an expert on project-based learning, just someone who's used it a lot. I'll just briefly mention some of the things I've learned about effectively guiding project-based learning.

When introducing the projects, set a clear tone that although the students have many options about what they do, you expect quality work and engagement no matter what they select. They might enjoy the work they do, but it will also be work, not just fun. As you introduce the projects, direct them in your expectations, especially about listening carefully and considering which option they take. Providing a graphic organizer with the project topics, a space to take notes, and a column for students to rate each project by their interest will help them listen productively to the introduction. You might give students a night to think about their projects, encouraging them to make a good decision. I always try to get across to my students that, because I'm giving them options, blaming me at the end with, "That project was so dumb!" isn't going to work. They need to choose wisely at this stage.

I typically require my students to work in groups. Managing one hundred or more students across all of your classes going in one hundred different directions is a difficult, if not impossible, task if you allow all of the students to work individually. If you have your students work in groups of three or four, then in each class you'll have probably five to eight projects going at once, and that's manageable. To do this, on the day I introduce the projects, I set students expectations by telling them that I will form project groups based on the project choices they make individually. They submit in writing up to three project options listed in order of which ones they are most interested in. I form the groups based on their preferences, always trying to give students their first or second choice.

I give my students two or three days of class time to get the work on their projects started. They need time together to work and plan, and I require written project plans from them. Typically, they make a table that shows in the left-most column the steps they will go through to accomplish their project. Column headers are the different group member's names. With that format, the cells in the table become spaces to show the specific task that each group member will work on in that step. Students need help dividing up labor fairly, and this type of table forces them to talk through who will do which job. Creating this table may take the whole first class period of the planning day. They submit the table, and I review it overnight to make sure their plan sounds reasonable and fair, writing down my comments. As the next day's project work begins, I give them back their project plans, have them review my comments first, and then make any needed revisions to their plan.

At the end of each planning day, I require a brief written report so that I can keep track of the groups and give them feedback. This update is also used to communicate individual homework assignments the students make for each other, which I check at the beginning of the next class to make sure each member is pulling his or her weight in the group. During class on each project workday, I move among the groups, helping them solve problems and conferencing with them briefly to improve their work.

After the initial two or three planning days, the students are ready to spend a few more days finalizing their projects, and much of this work has to been done individually. This is the point that project-based learning can feel like it eats into coverage of your overall curriculum, unless you've just covered the basics of evolution up until now and still have some more important content to cover. You can do this in two ways. The first is to have a scientific conference in which the students report on their efforts to continue learning about evolution as they work on their projects. You'll probably be surprised how much of the remaining essential content they actually figure out on their own as they pursue projects interesting to them. The second way to cover content is by teaching minilessons about important topics you've yet to touch on. Again, you'll probably be surprised about how naturally these come up. As you move around the room, listening to the students work on the projects, you may hear common confusion that you can solve by stopping all project work, teaching a ten- to fifteen-minute lesson that covers essential content and addresses their confusion, and then sending them back into their project work.

When the students are ready to present their work, I typically don't have them do formal presentations in front of the whole class. The first student presentation is often interesting, but by the third we're all losing interest, and by the sixth or seventh, it's just deadly boring. Unless my goal is to build students' skills for formal presentations, I tend toward a presentation session styled after scientific poster sessions. Each group (or individual) prepares a poster or a triboard overviewing the work they did, why they did it, their final product, and what they learned. We rearrange the desks for good traffic flow with everyone moving around the room, and the projects go on or against the walls. I then structure the presentation time so that the students move around the room, often at their own pace, to see their classmates' work. To keep them focused, I typically give them a graphic organizer to complete showing what they learn about their peers' work.

Alternatives to Project-Based Learning

I used a project-based approach to bring the unit back around to personal engagement, where inquiry begins in essential feature #1. If you don't want to use projects, then consider ways that you can help students exit the unit, connecting the content with their interests and values. This could be done in a well-crafted large-group discussion in which students talk about connections they are seeing. Students could write journal entries or other creative writing in which they describe the connections they see and then share those entries in small groups. Students could do Web-based research, find relevant examples, and report those via a small- or large-group discussion format.

Projects also allow students to pursue deeper answers about the content itself, especially aspects of evolution that particularly interest to them. If you elect not to use projects, you can still have students pursue deeper understandings. Each group could take one aspect of evolution, research it more deeply, and report their findings to the class. Students could form groups based on aspects of evolution that they're interested in, research their assigned topics, and summarize their findings briefly, including annotations, into PowerPoint presentations.

A final way to end the unit other than with projects involves having students fulfill essential feature #5 by organizing the work they did throughout the unit into a coherent whole, communicating a summary of the evidence for and explanation of evolution. This could be in the style of a formal paper if students need to develop their skills to make formal written arguments. This could also be by selecting and using a single graphic organizer that best matches the evidence and communicates the explanations from the unit to strengthen students' abilities to understand scientific arguments.

Ending the Unit

One of the most effective ways to end the unit is with students completing a final reflection on the unit's essential question. Bringing the students back to where they started brings them a sense of closure and helps them finalize their understandings. You can keep this process brief by simply having a large-group discussion in which a few students talk out their new understandings of why studying evolution is important. You could also ask students to review their work throughout the unit, giving them time to write their responses. Then they would meet with a peer to discuss what they have written. Finally, you would orally collect a summary of their responses by asking several students who are willing to describe for the class what they have written about how their thinking has changed in the unit.

8 Wrapping Up

I really had no idea how pivotal seeing Lucy would be, both for me personally and for writing this book. My faith teaches me to believe in Providence, and now, looking back, I see how providential that experience in Houston was. Evolution can be so scary for many theistic people, but when I saw Lucy, as I describe in the Introduction, I was ready more than ever to understand what she had to teach me without feeling it would threaten my faith. Hopefully, your evolution unit will function in similar ways for your students as inquiry provides the missing link between resistant students and a solid understanding of evolution.

Many of your students are scared of evolution, just as I was. I was scared of everything about evolution in ninth grade. I was intimidated by the evidence for human evolution before I met Lucy, and there are still areas that concern me as I think about looking even more deeply into the evidence for evolution. You can't know the end result of your unit for your resistant students. Some might walk away from your unit simply less scared of evolution because of the gentle way you've lead them in inquiry on the evidence for evolution. That in itself is good progress.

Others may also increase their understanding of evolution, either a little bit or a lot. I didn't understand evolution when I was in school, and my fears of evolution caused me to hold it off at a distance so that I never could actually gather the right understandings. As I've realized that looking at evolution, like my visit to Lucy, doesn't necessarily require me to change my beliefs, I've been able to deepen my understanding of evolution and recognize misunderstandings I have. I'm now more comfortable than ever learning about evolution. Your students should walk away from your unit with a more solid understanding of evolution than I ever had as a student because inquiry will guide them to build their own understandings and your sensitive accommodations will allow them to learn without fear that you're going to challenge their beliefs. Combining better understanding with less fear, your students will also be poised to continue building their understandings as they move into life beyond your course. They'll be less afraid to take a biology course when they're in college, read about evolution in a magazine, or watch a Discovery Channel show focusing on evolution.

Looking Back

What do I hope you've heard in this book? I've covered a lot of territory. You've examined many sample lesson plans, each with multiple accommodation strategies for resistant students. You've looked at many online resources, including those showing the evidence that is piling up for evolution. You've read about the many different tensions theistic students face when learning evolution is required in their science classes. I hope you walk away with a few big ideas that you can hold onto as you stand before your students and teach your unit.

First, consider implementing more inquiry-based approaches to teaching evolution. That in itself will diffuse some of the conflict. If you stand in front of your students and require that they learn evolution because you're an authority figure, even if you are trying to represent the authority of science, you run the risk of students challenging you based on the power of their beliefs. When that happens, we're back to the old question without answer: "Which is right—science or religion?" Instead, by beginning first with the evidence, as inquiry requires, you're putting in front of students the facts from which scientists have built the theory of evolution. You're not asking them to accept that evolution is true because you say so. Instead, you're asking them to build their understandings based on a foundation of actual evidence.

Consider implementing more the key teacher role in inquiry-based instruction: guiding students in developing the ability to build scientific explanations from evidence. If you're used to giving lectures to students, then this aspect of inquiry may be a new way to look at teaching and learning. Rather than telling students how to interpret the evidence, instead guide them in interpreting the evidence, making sure that their explanations eventually match the accepted ideas of science. As a part of this aspect of teaching by inquiry, consider the distinction between natural and supernatural explanations as a key strategy in engaging resistant students in learning evolution without threatening their deep beliefs. Don't ask them to accept that evolution explains the evidence. Instead, ask them to understand how scientists explain the evidence with Darwin's theory when they limit themselves to only natural explanations.

Consider how this approach treats your resistant students and the conflicts they feel with a high level of dignity and respect. You don't have to ignore their beliefs, as some science teachers do when they teach evolution. Those beliefs are at the core of our theistic students, and ignoring their faith denies dignity to a central part of who they are and what they bring to the science classroom. But don't ignore evolution, either, leaving it out of your course as some science teachers do. Ignoring evolution leaves students unprepared for a world in which they will consistently encounter evolution.

As a reminder, this book doesn't present an entire set of lessons for your evolution unit. The lessons here give you examples of how to teach evolution by inquiry and how to teach it so that more resistant students are engaged. You will need to add other lessons, either ones you have previously taught or ones you create, in order to give your students the breadth and depth of understanding they need.

"What Do You Believe?"

How much should we as teachers talk to our students about our own personal beliefs? This is a question that I hear often from teachers when we discuss teaching evolution. Deciding how to answer your students when they ask, "What do you believe?" is tough, and I don't have quick, clean advice for you. Instead, I'll lay out some of the issues involved and tell you what I do regarding talking about my own beliefs.

I waited until this final chapter to address this issue to model how you can go through the whole unit on evolution without talking about your own personal beliefs. Throughout this book, I haven't talked much about the specifics of my beliefs, but you were still able to understand what I had to say about evolution and how students should learn it. In the same way, you don't have to talk about your beliefs with your students in order for them to learn. You can simply say something like, "Actually, I don't think it's a good idea for me to talk about what I believe." One of the most important reasons for doing so is the weight of authority that you carry in the classroom. Students with beliefs similar to yours might have a tendency simply to accept your beliefs about evolution without thinking the issues through. Students with beliefs different than yours might feel the need to balance any statements you make about your beliefs by talking about their own beliefs. Your authority may confuse the issue, and students can understand evolution without knowing what you believe.

Also, consider how this approach to teaching evolution guides you to deemphasize talk about beliefs. The point of your instruction is student understanding, not belief. You're not asking students to accept evolution; so, in many ways, when students ask you what you believe, they're asking the wrong question. I guided you in the final portion of your unit to let your theistic students select projects by which they could explore the interface of their faith and evolution, but that's advice only for a few students and only for a small portion of the unit. For most of your unit, your answer is simply along the lines of, "Belief isn't in question here. Not mine and not yours. Your beliefs and mine are very important, but our focus in class is on understanding evolution, not who believes in it and who doesn't." You've probably seen students who like to sidetrack a lesson on the science of evolution with a discussion on who believes what. Deemphasizing discussions of belief keeps the focus on scientific understandings, which is both your job and the students' work in your class.

Please carefully think through your legal duty to avoid establishing any one religion if you do choose to talk about your beliefs. Some teachers tell their students what they believe, and in certain settings that works. Public schools must not establish religion, however, and this is an area where caution is important, especially because children can think you are pushing your beliefs on them even if you aren't. Be cautious—if you speak of your beliefs, you might unduly influence students, because you have authority. To be just, if you talk about your beliefs during class, you should commit yourself to allowing students to express their own beliefs as well. You might say something to the effect of, "You've heard what I believe. Now, I want to hear from you. What are your beliefs?" In my view, you then have to be serious about wanting them to express their beliefs, and you have to be willing to dedicate the time required for your students to talk about the range of their beliefs. Opening the floor for all students to talk about their beliefs is an indicator to them that you're not trying to establish your beliefs as those that are right and true. As you can imagine, though, there are multiple problems with this approach. You're at the very least diverting time away from the science curriculum. You also could be opening yourself up to legal challenge if a student's family members perceives you as trying to impose your beliefs on their son or daughter.

Many teachers may choose to talk about their personal beliefs but only outside of class, especially if students seek them out. Talking outside of class is a better way to avoid the charge of establishing any one religion and the sense that you are imposing your beliefs on your students. In class, a teacher following this approach might say, "My beliefs are very important to me, but I don't talk about them during class. I'm happy to talk with you about them outside of class, though, if you'd like to come see me." If students see you after school hours, then you have some controls in place that you aren't coercing the students to believe what you do, especially because they can leave if they become uncomfortable with what you're saying. This out-of-class relationship can take on a mentoring aspect, either for students with beliefs similar to yours who are looking for a role model or for students who are curious about your beliefs and want to know more.

Looking Ahead

Following is the approach that I use in talking about my personal beliefs with my students. My faith is at the very core of who I am, and it gives me great hope. I don't understand all of the interface between science and my beliefs, but because I believe in God, I find myself pondering how God may have used evolution to create this stunningly beautiful world. I'm still on a journey of learning. So, in a similar fashion to the last approach, I just told you a bit of my beliefs, and I now invite you to talk to me "outside of class." Please seek me out. Maybe you can help me along my journey of understanding and belief, and I can do the same for you.

I also would like to hear how this approach to teaching evolution helps you to better teach your students, especially your resistant students. As I said in the Introduction, I know that you'll tweak and modify and reinvent the lessons and approaches that I've described here. That's what we teachers do, right? We take a good idea and make it our own, and that's what I hope you will do with what I've written. Please use this book as a springboard to find the classroom approaches that work well for you and your students. I'd be especially curious to hear from you examples of your students' work as you implement this approach and your stories of the ways in which you've been able to be more successful with your resistant students.

In the last few weeks of finishing this book, Barack Obama was inaugurated as the forty-fourth president of the United States, and I was reminded in a powerful way about the hope of truly open doors. I found myself wondering how many American children of color watched the inauguration and said to themselves, "I really *can* grow up to be president!" In a similar fashion, one of my long-felt passions has been that more theistic students would see science as a place that they can fit into, without having to deny or downplay their faith. We need the diversity of all people, including all religions, doing science, and we need the diversity of all students learning about science, including evolution. Evolution doesn't have to drive theistic students out of science careers or even keep students from simply appreciating science as they go about theirs lives after their science studies end.

As we find approaches to teaching evolution that don't require children necessarily to change what they believe, we'll reduce the controversy in the classroom, help students to understand what science is and isn't, and see more resistant students learning science. My biggest hope is that we'll then see more students walking through newly opened doors and finding their calling in science.

Appendix: Help! I'm a Biology Teacher, and I Don't Think I Understand Evolution Myself!

If you find yourself teaching evolution without confidence that you really understand it well yourself, working through the material in this Appendix will help you. Maybe you grew up in a faith that saw conflict with evolution; therefore, you didn't learn evolution well as you went through school. You may still be of a faith in which you currently experience conflict with evolution; therefore, studying evolution continues to be difficult for you. You may be coming to your job as a teacher of evolution from a different field, either a different science certification area or from outside of science teaching itself; therefore, you need to build your first solid understandings of evolution. Whatever the reason, this Appendix is designed to help you deepen your understanding of evolution so that you guide your students effectively in their inquiries about evolution.

You'll examine evidence from three areas foundational to understanding evolution, especially with reference to common objections about evolution. One objection you have probably heard is, "Well, there really isn't any evidence of new species evolving, right?" To help you better understand that issue, I'll guide you through the evidence for the evolution of whales from a land-dwelling mammal. Another objection is the long amount of time involved, and this objection resonates with many theistic people. You'll hear people say, "The Earth really isn't that old, despite what scientists say. Besides, you can't really trust carbon-14 dating. It's not accurate." I'll guide you in the scientific evidence that gives us confidence that C_{14} and other radiometric techniques are trustworthy. I'll also guide you to examine the evidence for human evolution, a third common objection and one again heard among many theistic people.

As you can imagine, I can't cover all of the evidence for evolution here. Instead, the three areas I've chosen represent some of the key concepts that support evolution as a one of the really big ideas of science. These three key concepts also intersect with each other. Evolution requires vast amounts of time, and radiometric dating provides the evidence that whale, human, and other fossils are truly old. The evolution of whales provides scientific confidence that new species really have appeared in the fossil record, a confidence that can then be applied to the evidence for human evolution and other species. The evidence for human evolution reminds us that all of our discussions, including those of new species and the time required for evolution to occur, can be done by looking at the evidence to understand how the scientific community has made its current conclusions with natural explanations for the evidence they find.

Perhaps you've jumped into this Appendix before you've read much of the rest of the book. If so, let me preview one of the key points the book makes. Your goal as you read this should be understanding the evidence and how scientists explain it, but you don't necessarily have to accept those conclusions. That's the essence of the approach to teaching evolution detailed in the rest of the book. Scientists at all points on the belief spectrum, from deeply spiritual to atheistic, have found their place working in the scientific community. In the same way, teachers from all across the spectrum of beliefs can teach evolution effectively.

Whale Evolution

A key objection to evolution runs along the lines of, "Well, there's just no proof that new species ever evolved. Sure, I believe natural selection occurs, but there's no proof that one species ever changed into a different species." Evidence countering this objection is piling up, and whale evolution is one clear example. The chain of evidence for the evolution of whales now has all of the major links in it. Examining the evidence for whale evolution will give you one strong reference point in your teaching for how scientists explain the evolution of new species.

As you look at the fossil series leading to modern whales laid out, you can clearly see the evidence for the change from a land-dwelling common ancestor (*Pakicetus*) to modern whales. With a little bit of filtering, you can find a lot of good information on whale evolution with a Google search. Following are some of the sites that I found the most helpful to me in better understanding the evolution of whales. As you review these, keep in mind that you are looking to build your understanding of the evidence for whale evolution and how scientists explain that evidence with natural explanations. The evolution of whales is not proof that the supernatural wasn't involved in the evolution of whales. Following the limits of science (see Chapter 6), supernatural involvement is simply an issue that paleontologists can't address in their work, either to prove or disprove any role that supernatural forces may have played.

- "Whale Origins Research," a website[1] from the lab of paleontologist J. G. M. "Hans" Thewissen (Google keywords: Thewissen whale origins research)

  This website was the best presentation of this chain of evidence I found online. At the site, you can click on the different branches of the family tree of whales to see the fossil evidence for each branch. Doing this was helpful to me because I could see clearly the evidence for the anatomic changes during the evolution of whales, especially the disappearance of legs.

- "Evidence for Evolution" section[2] of WGBH's Evolution Library (Google keywords: WGBH evolution library)

  WGBH's Evolution website is the best starting point for almost all of my searches for teaching evolution. In the "Evidence for Evolution" section of the library are several resources that focus on whale evolution, as well as many giving the evidence for evolution in general.

---

[1]http://www.neoucom.edu/DEPTS/ANAT/Thewissen/whale_origins/index.html.
[2]www.pbs.org/wgbh/evolution/library/04/index.html.

The video clip "Evolving Ideas: How Do We Know Evolution Happens?" uses the evolution of whales to talk about evolution in general. That section of the evolution library also gives other resources on whale evolution, some of which are online.

- "Evolution: Fossils, Genes, and Mousetraps," a lecture[3] by Kenneth Miller (Google keywords: HHMI mousetraps)

  In a lecture to high school students, Kenneth Miller, Ph.D., gives an excellent overview of how gaps in the fossil record are being filled in with new research, using whale evolution as an example. The visuals he uses are especially useful. A DVD of the lecture is available free by ordering from Howard Hughes Medical Institute, at the link above, and his lecture on whales is in Chapter 10 of the DVD. You may also find the lecture online by searching a service such as YouTube, where it will be helpful to know that his comments on whales occur at about twenty minutes into the 1.5 hour lecture. Dr. Miller points out how with time, the work of paleontologists continues to fill in gaps in the fossil record, and during his lecture he shows contrasting visuals illustrating this point, which was most helpful to me. The evidence truly is piling up, just as Darwin's theory would predict.

- "The Evolution of Whales, Adapted from National Geographic, November 2001," a website[4] by Edward Babinski (Google keywords: Babinski "the whale tale")

  Douglas Chadwick's article "The Evolution of Whales" from *National Geographic* in November 2002 is an excellent treatment of whale evolution. Edward T. Babinski has posted a good overview of whale evolution, basing his work on Chadwick's article. The coverage of whale evolution in both publications keeps the description grounded in the evidence by consistently bringing in the relevant fossils while sweeping through the story of whale evolution.

---

[3] www.hhmi.org/catalog/main?action=product&itemId=323.
[4] www.edwardtbabinski.us/whales/evolution_of_whales/.

- "Research on the Origin and Early Evolution of Whales," a website[5] compiling the research of Philip D. Gingerich (Google keyword: Gingerich early evolution)

Philip D. Gingerich is the paleontologist featured in the "Evolving Ideas" video mentioned above at the WGBH evolution library. His site shows in time line form the contribution of his research to the understanding of whale evolution, including pictures of the fossils coming out of the ground. These pictures were a helpful reminder to me that fossils don't just appear! Instead, the fossil record for a species becomes complete only after paleontologists do the painstaking work of locating and unearthing the fossils. A special feature of the site is links to almost all of his research studies, if you want to dig into the evidence as presented to the scientific community.

Deep Time and Radiometric Dating

The scale of time involved in evolution is hard for most people to grasp. Evolution works over a span of millions of years, and grasping that kind of sweep of time requires a good deal of intellectual work. Understanding these time scales is made more difficult if people's faith teaches them that the Earth is only a few thousand years old. Understanding the evidence for these long sweeps of time will give you foundational knowledge for teaching evolution and more confidence in the different disciplines of science supporting Darwin's theory.

Some scientists call the amount of time involved in evolution "deep time," picking up on astronomers' references to deep space. I stumbled around on the Internet as I tried to understand deep time better until I began using the search term "radiometric dating." Searching other terms, especially "carbon dating," wasn't very productive for me. As I looked at the science, I saw clear evidence for the millions of years required for evolution of life on Earth. But, I also kept in mind that understanding these scientific

[5]www-personal.umich.edu/~gingeric/PDGwhales/Whales.htm.

ideas doesn't mean giving up belief in the supernatural. Deep time is a scientific explanation constructed within the rules that all scientific explanations must employ only natural explanations.

- The "Deep Time/History of the Earth" section[6] of WGBH's Evolution Library (Google keywords: WGBH evolution library)

  The "Deep Time/History of the Earth" section of WGBH'S evolution library provides good jumping-off points for increasing your understanding of the scientific evidence for the length of time involved in evolution. I found the "Deep Time" Web activity very helpful. It's interactive, so I could go at my own pace as I tried to see the connections between geological changes, biological evolution, and extinction of species. The video "Radiometric Dating" gives a quick introduction of how scientists date rocks via radioactive decay.

- "Claim CD010: Radiometric dating gives unreliable results," a website[7] from TalkOrigins (Google search: talk origins index, scroll down to "CD: Geology," then click on Claim CD010)

  I try to steer clear of the creation/evolution controversy whenever I can. It's a dead-end discussion to me, but I do find the TalkOrigins Archive (http://talkorigins.org/) helpful at times. Even though the information on radiometric dating is written as a rebuttal of creationist claims, it helped me build my understanding of radiometric dating because of the quick, concise overview and the links provided to online scientific articles. As always, these scientific perspectives don't disprove the supernatural, but they help show how radiometric dating is part of the natural explanation of origins that scientists have constructed.

- "Radiometric Dating: A Christian Perspective," a website[8] with content authored by Dr. Roger C. Wiens (Google keywords: Christian radiometric dating)

---

[6]www.pbs.org/wgbh/evolution/library/03/index.html.
[7]http://talkorigins.org/indexcc/CD/CD010.html.
[8]www.asa3.org/aSA/resources/Wiens.html.

Again, I try to stay away from the war between creationists and scientific materialists, but I have found a resource written directly to a creationist Christian audience helpful. I have heard many objections raised by creationists, and I was confused by some of them. Dr. Weins' paper gently, but directly, addressed many of those from the standpoint of scientific evidence. He lays out a case for the validity of radiometric dating, including a good description of each technique.

- "Geologic Time," a website[9] from the U.S. Geological Survey (Google keywords: geologic time USGS)

  The U.S. Geological Survey offers a resource giving a quick walk across the big ideas of geological time. It helped me see why radiometric dating is essential in understanding evolution. This website also helped me expand my understanding of the dating of ancient materials beyond simply C_{14} dating. It's been a long time since I studied geology, and I had forgotten that different isotopes are more appropriate for samples from different geologic periods.

- "Web Geological Time Machine," a website[10] from the University of California Museum of Paleontology (Google search: geological time machine)

  If you've forgotten much of your geology, as I have, then you might need a good review. The connections between geology and biology are essential understandings, because biological evolution occurred within the context of geological evolution. The site is particularly helpful because of the examples of actual fossil evidence that it includes as "Ancient Life" links for many of the geological periods.

---

[9]http://pubs.usgs.gov/gip/geotime/contents.html.

[10]www.ucmp.berkeley.edu/help/timeform.html.

Human Evolution

Human evolution is where things get really uncomfortable for many people. At first blush, evolution seems to say that we humans are just animals and maybe even just bits of cosmic luck, when the human experience tells so many of us that we are much more than just products of random genetic mutations. As a secondary science teacher, you need to understand the evidence for human evolution so that you can adequately field questions that your students raise, even though you probably won't teach human evolution to your classes. Neither your students nor you, if you have certain beliefs, have to abandon your faith, including beliefs about humans being created specially by supernatural events. As with the others aspects of evolution, the main criteria are that you understand the scientific evidence for human evolution and how scientists explain that evidence using only natural explanations.

- The "Human Evolution" section[11] of WGBH's Evolution Library (Google keywords: WGBH evolution library)

  The fossil evidence for humanlike species continues to pile up. The fossil record linking all primates to a common ancestor is filling in, and the phylogenetic tree of humanlike species is being tied down by clear scientific evidence. The WGBH Evolution site provides a great jumping-off point for research on human evolution. The "Human Evolution" portion contains several good resources that are either located or linked from there. I found all of the subsequent resources, other than the Lucy Exhibition at the Houston Museum of Natural Sciences. The video clip "Finding Lucy" at the WGBH site provides a nice overview of the paleontology involved in the discovery of *Australopithecus afarensis*, a key transitional species in the chain of evidence involved in human evolution. The "Origins of Humankind" Web activity was helpful to me by providing a self-paced, interactive

---

[11]www.pbs.org/wgbh/evolution/library/07/index.html.

format for building my understanding of human evolution with actual evidence.

■ "Lucy's Legacy: Hidden Treasures of Ethiopia," a website[12] from the Houston Museum of Natural Science (Google keywords: lucy exhibition)

Lucy is probably the most famous prehuman skeleton discovered. As I described in the Introduction, I was instantly aware that this was clear evidence for human evolution when I saw her bones at the Houston Museum of Natural Science. I was unaware, however, until I saw the Lucy Exhibition that the scientific argument for human evolution focused on Lucy's knees and how their structure shows that Lucy's species is a transitional form between modern humans and the common ancestor of all primates. Reviewing this argument will help you to understand the logical flow scientists use in linking together the chain of evidence involved in human evolution.

■ "Fossil Hominids: The Evidence for Human Evolution," a website[13] from talkorigins.org (Google keywords: talkorigins fossil hominids)

As I mentioned earlier, even though TalkOrigins is a website involved in the creation/evolution wars, I still find some of their resources useful. I needed to brush up on my human paleontology, and the "Hominid Species" and "Hominid Fossils" pages of this site helped me to get a clearer sense of humans' phylogenetic tree. The site gives good details on the evidence for human evolution, but most of it is text based and not actual pictures of evidence. So, the site focuses on the explanations of science, but it doesn't link directly the evidence from which those explanations have been built.

■ "The Human Origins Program," a website[14] from the Smithsonian Institution (Google keywords: Smithsonian human origins)

---

[12]http://lucyexhibition.com.
[13]www.toarchive.org/faqs/homs/.
[14]http://anthropology.si.edu/humanorigins.

The Smithsonian Institution is building and putting online an extensive collection of prehuman fossils, and I was impressed that the long-term mission of their website is to build a complete online collection. The site gives actual evidence because you can look at images of the fossils. In fact, you can even revolve some of the skulls in the Hall of Human Evidence to view them from all sides. From the Hall's welcome page click the "Go to Human Family Tree" link to the page entitled "Early Human Phylogeny," which was especially helpful to me. It shows the typical phylogenetic tree for human origin, but it's interactive. Don't miss on that page how many of the bars representing transitional species are clickable links to photographs of evidence specimens from the Smithsonian collection.

- "Becoming Human," a website (http://becominghuman.org) from The Institute of Human Origins

An interactive website from the Institute of Human Origins may help you see the bigger picture of human evolution without getting lost in the details. The strengths of this site are its focus on the scientific explanations of human origins and the interactive nature of the site itself. It is weak on actual evidence, however, focusing mostly on the explanations scientists offer for human evolution.

Summary

The resources you've examined here should give you more confidence about both content and process. From a content perspective, it should be clear that the evidence base for evolution continues to build and that evolution itself makes good sense within the limits of science restricting explanations to natural causes. From a process perspective, I hope that you see that the evidence for evolution isn't necessarily threatening, especially when you consider that understanding evolution doesn't require you or your students to abandon your faith. I also hope you see that a wealth of resources exists to help you better understand evolution, especially actual evidence available online that you can reference when you have questions or concerns about teaching evolution.

You may also want to consider using these resources with your students. Some of the resources are already built into lessons outlines given in this book. Other resources referenced here may help you design your own lessons, especially those that you need to flesh out your evolution unit beyond the basic lessons I present. You may also want to consider referring some of these resources to individual students, based on their unique needs or questions.

Discussion Questions for Study Groups

Getting the Group Started (Introduction)

- You have read Dr. Meadows' story about meeting Lucy. What story can you tell that describes your experiences with learning evolution as a student yourself?
- What story can you tell to share your typical experience with teaching evolution to classes with resistant students?
- As you look at the chapter topics and key questions (Table I.1), what do you look forward to about the book? What concerns do you have about what is ahead?

Understanding Evolution (Appendix)

Note that your group needs to decide whether you want to discuss the material in the Appendix and, if so, when. Discussion questions from the Appendix are included here before the questions for the other chapters mainly as a reminder that working through the Appendix material now may be helpful to your group.

- How confident are you about your own understanding of evolution? Evaluate the instruction you received about evolution when you were a student.

- What questions do you have about whale evolution? Which resources given in the Appendix are most helpful to you?
- What questions do you have about radiometric dating and deep time? Which resources given in the Appendix are most helpful to you?
- What questions do you have about human evolution? Will you bring up human evolution with your students?
- Which resources in the Appendix would be helpful to your students?

Discussing the Issues (Chapter 1)

- What is your initial response to the idea of teaching evolution to resistant students so that they understand it, but don't necessarily accept it?
- This book takes a strong stand that evolution is essential content that students must learn. Do you agree? Why or why not?
- How do you respond to what Chapter 1 says about valuing our students' beliefs?
- How have you used inquiry-based science teaching in your classroom? What is your reaction to the idea of using inquiry to teach evolution?

Focusing Your Unit (Chapter 2)

- What is your reaction to the overall strategy for planning a unit? How is it different from how you plan? How is it similar?
- How helpful to you is the "Explaining Evolution" map from *Atlas of Science Literacy* in thinking about the big ideas you want your students to learn in your unit?
- How do Tables 2.1, 2.2, and 2.3 help you to think about the content you want your students to learn?
- How might your final unit focus differ from what is presented in Table 2.4 (middle school teachers) or Table 2.5 (high school teachers)?

- Chapter 2 suggests the essential question "Why can't we just skip evolution?" Discuss possible alternatives to essential questions. Which essential question would be the most productive for your students?

Engaging Students in Evolution (Chapter 3)

- How do you try to engage your students in the science content? What strategies work for you? What is difficult about engaging students in studying science?
- When you read the description of theistic students, do individual students come to mind, either from your current or previous students? What problems do theistic students have when studying evolution?
- Which of the engaging experiences described in Chapter 3 would be most successful with your students?
- What questions and concerns do you have as you examine the lesson segments described in Tables 3.1, 3.2, and 3.3? Which parts of those lesson segments will your students respond well to?
- Review the Typical Objections to Evolution and think about the objections your resistant students might raise. What concerns do you have?

Guiding Students to Examine the Evidence for Evolution (Chapter 4)

- What is your initial reaction (overwhelmed? excited? confused?) as you read through Chapter 4 and think about beginning the study of evolution with students by examining the evidence for evolution?
- How might your students respond to the lesson on natural selection given in Table 4.1? What would work well for them? What would be challenging?
- How might your students respond to the lesson on the evidence for evolution given in Table 4.2? What would work well for them? What would be challenging?

- Discuss the accommodations for theistic students given in both lessons in Chapter 4. What new approaches to working with resistant students are there? What concerns do you have about the accommodations? How will your students respond if you implemented those accommodations?

Guiding Students to Examine Evolution (Chapter 5)

- How much have you thought about the difference between natural and supernatural explanations? What questions do you have about the distinction? How can you use the differences to ease the tensions resistant students face when learning about evolution?
- What questions do you have about whale evolution? Discuss any questions you have about the lesson on whale evolution.
- What questions do you have about HIV evolution? Discuss any questions you have about the lesson on HIV evolution.
- What questions do you have about bird evolution? Discuss any questions you have about the lesson on bird evolution.
- Discuss the accommodations for theistic students given in the lessons in Chapter 5. How will your students respond to those accommodations?

Deepening Understanding/ Addressing Objections (Chapter 6)

- Inquiry requires you to craft effective large-group discussions with your students as they process the evidence put in front of them. What is working in your classroom as you try to implement those types of discussions? What is challenging?
- How might your students respond to the scientific worldview lesson given in Table 6.1? What value will they get out of it? What will be challenging about guiding them through this lesson?

- Discuss the approach to dealing with objections described in Chapter 6. What aspects of the approach sound most beneficial for your students? How might you modify the approach to best meet the needs of your students?

Solidifying Student Understanding (Chapter 7)

- How well are your students learning evolution? Are they getting the big ideas given in Tables 2.1, 2.2, and 2.3?
- How have you used project-based learning in the past? If you have, what works for you about the approach? If you have not, what concerns do you have about it?
- Which of the projects in Table 7.1 will be most beneficial for your students in helping them finalize their understandings of evolution? What will be challenging about guiding their work in those projects?
- Which of the projects in Table 7.2 will be most beneficial for your theistic students in helping them finalize their understandings of evolution? What will be challenging about guiding their work in those projects? How do you feel about the set of projects specifically tailored to the unique needs of your theistic students?
- Examine the alternatives to project-based learning. Which of these are you considering? What other alternatives will help your students exit the unit with a solid understand of evolution?

Wrapping Up (Chapter 8)

- Review the big ideas in the Looking Back section of Chapter 8. What is the most important lesson you learned from reading this book? Is there a big lesson you learned that is not mentioned in the section?
- How will you answer a student who asks, "What do you believe?" How does this section of the book help you to think through the issues involved in answering questions about your beliefs?

■ Scan the last paragraph. How are you doing with opening the door to science for all of your students? What about specifically with your resistant students?

References

AMERICAN ASSOCIATION FOR THE ADVANCEMENT OF SCIENCE. 1993. *Benchmarks for Science Literacy*. Available at: www.project2061.org/publications/bsl/online/bolintro.htm.

BRANSFORD, JOHN D., ANN L. BROWN, and RODNEY D. COCKING, eds. 1999. *How People Learn: Brain, Mind, Experience, & School*. Washington, DC: National Academy Press. Available at: http://books.nap.edu/catalog.php?record_id=6160.

COVEY, STEPHEN R. 1989. *The 7 Habits of Highly Effective People: Powerful Lessons in Personal Change.* New York: Fireside Books.

DOBZHANSKY, THEODOSIUS. 1973. "Nothing in Biology Makes Sense Except in the Light of Evolution." *The American Biology Teacher* (35): 125–29.

EICK, CHARLES, LEE MEADOWS, and REBECCA BALKCOM. 2005. "Breaking into Inquiry: Scaffolding Supports Beginning Efforts to Implement Inquiry in the Classroom." *The Science Teacher* (October): 49–53.

FREEMAN, SCOTT, and HERRON, JON C. 2004. Evolutionary Analysis. Upper Saddle River, NJ: Pearson Prentice Hall.

McCARTHY, BERNICE. 2000. *About Teaching: 4MAT in the Classroom.* Wauconda, IL: About Learning.

MEADOWS, LEE. 2007. "Teacher Knowledge About Inquiry: Incorporating Conceptual Change Theory." In: Eleanor Abrams, Sherry A. Southerland, and Peggy Silva, editors. *Inquiry in the Classroom: Reality and Opportunities.* Charlotte, NC: Information Age Publishing.

———. 2008. "Change in Secondary Science Settings: A Voice from the Field." In: Julie Gess-Newsome, Julie A. Luft, and Randy Bell, editors. *Reforming Secondary Science Instruction.* Washington, DC: National Science Teachers Association.

National Academy of Sciences and Institute of Medicine. 2008. *Science, Evolution, and Creationism.* Washington, DC: The National Academies Press. Available at: http://books.nap.edu/catalog.php?record_id=11876.

National Research Council. 1996. *National Science Education Standards.* Washington, DC: National Academy Press.

———. 2000. *Inquiry and the National Science Education Standards: A Guide for Teaching and Learning.* Washington, DC: National Academy Press. Available at: http://books.nap.edu/catalog.php?record_id=9596.

Project 2061. 2001. *Atlas of Science Literacy.* Washington, DC: American Association for the Advancement of Science, National Science Teachers Association.

Rutherford, James, and Andrew Ahlgren. 1990. *Science for All Americans.* New York: Oxford University Press. Available at: www.project2061.org/publications/sfaa/online/sfaatoc.htm.

Wiggins, G., and Jay McTighe. 2005. *Understanding by Design,* expanded 2d ed. Saddle River, NJ: Prentice Hall.